CELEBRATING HERBS

Cooking Arts Collection™

NTRODUCTION

Fragrant, attractive and sometimes mysterious, herbs are perhaps the most seductive of all the ingredients used in cooking. While seldom featured as primary ingredients, herbs impart an essential flavor dimension to a dish and give it a distinctive personality.

Herbs have become more prominent on the North American culinary scene and, happily, more accessible to the home cook. Today's supermarkets stock a good selection of fresh herbs throughout the year. During the growing season, garden centers offer a dazzling array to tempt the kitchen gardener. As this book demonstrates, you can grow your own herbs. And thanks to overnight shipping, you can purchase some of the more exotic herbs, such as angelica and lovage, by mail order.

When I left for Paris to study cooking about 25 years ago, my exposure to herbs was limited to curly parsley and dried seasonings from a bottle. At La Varenne cooking school, I was introduced to the classic pairing of fresh tarragon and chicken, and learned to love the tart flavor of sorrel in soup or in sauce for fish. In spring and summer, there was always a generous supply of fresh chervil to garnish salads. During winter, we bundled parsley stems, dried thyme sprigs and bay leaves into fat *bouquet garnis* to flavor the hearty braises and stocks that simmered constantly at the back of the *fourneau* (stove).

My formal training is in classic French cooking, but in the years since my stint in Paris, I have enjoyed traveling and learning about the cuisines from many places. While exploring ethnic cooking, I have discovered some particularly interesting and effective uses of herbs. I have always been charmed by the way Southeast Asian cooks finish a salad or soup with a generous shower of vibrant cilantro, mint or basil. In Greek cooking, *avgolemono* — a mixture of egg, lemon juice and dill — adds a magical touch to soups and stews. Navigating the world of herbs provides a fascinating opportunity for a global taste tour.

In addition to developing more adventurous dining habits, many of us have become more concerned with eating healthfully. Relying on herbs for flavor is one of the easiest and most delicious ways to enjoy a healthier diet. In this collection you will find numerous recipes that are inherently healthful because they derive their complex flavor from herbs rather than fat- and sodium-laden ingredients. The recipes are not stingy with beneficial fats, such as olive oil and nuts, but use a minimum of saturated fat. When it comes to creating flavorful — yet healthful — food, not only are herbs a cook's best friends, they are strategic allies as well.

The art of cooking with herbs ranges from a suggestion to a bold statement. Lavender, for example, is exquisite when used subtly, offering just a hint of its presence. Basil, on the other hand, can be used with abandon and happily asserts itself in pesto sauce and tomato salads. The recipes in *Celebrating Herbs* illustrate these principles. My goal is to show you how to use herbs in varied and exciting ways, in dishes ranging from appetizers and breads to main courses and desserts.

The fresh taste of herbs is something to celebrate. As you learn more about these valuable seasonings, I hope you will experiment with some unfamiliar herbs in your cooking and enjoy everyday herbs in delicious and sometimes surprising ways.

HERB ESSENTIALS

What is the best way to store herbs? How can you preserve herbs? When should you add them to a recipe? In this chapter, you will find answers to these questions, plus many interesting tricks, such as how to turn a lemongrass stalk into a skewer for grilling.

Edible Flowers, page 17

TIPS AND TECHNIQUES FOR PREPARING HERBS

Cooking creatively with herbs starts with proper cleaning, storage and preparation techniques. Here are the secrets.

STORING SHORT-TERM

In an ideal world, you would always harvest herbs just before using them. But in real life, you will often need to store bunches of herbs in the refrigerator for a few days. Here are several options:

Bouquet of Flowers Method. Leafy, tender herbs — such as parsley and dill — are well-suited to this method. Trim stem ends, place herb stems in a container of water, cover loosely with a plastic bag and refrigerate. Most herbs will keep for up to 1 week; change water every 2 days.

Plastic Food Bag Method. Supermarket herbs are often subjected to produce misting to keep them looking good in the store. But because moisture promotes rotting, it is a good idea to wrap herbs in paper towels to absorb moisture before enclosing in a plastic food-storage bag. Herbs protected in this way and stored in the vegetable crisper should keep for up to 4 days, depending on freshness and type of herb. Plastic bags specially designed for extending the storage time of fruits and vegetables are useful for fresh herbs. These reusable, breathable bags are processed with the mineral oya, which absorbs ethylene gas. They can be found in health food stores.

Note that basil turns black when refrigerated. Use as soon as possible after harvesting or purchasing.

CLEANING

Sturdy herbs and some packaged herbs require just a thorough rinse under cold water and patting dry with a paper towel. But large bunches of parsley, basil, cilantro and dill may harbor grit, so wash them carefully as you would salad greens. Strip leaves from stems. Place leaves in a salad spinner basket and set it in the basin of a salad spinner. (Or use a colander set in a large bowl.) Fill the basket with cold water and swish. Let soak for a few minutes, then lift out the basket. Repeat the process until no trace of grit remains in the basin. Spin herbs dry. It is important to dry herbs thoroughly before storing or chopping.

STRIPPING LEAVES FROM STEMS

In most cases, it is the leaves you want to use in cooking. For herbs like parsley, cilantro, basil and dill, grasp the stems and pull off the leaves. To strip leaves from thyme, oregano, savory and tarragon, grasp sprigs at the top and run your fingers along the stem toward its base.

TEARING

Tender herbs, such as basil and chervil, are lovely when simply torn into small pieces. This casual approach is appropriate for dishes such as tomato salads and green salads.

SNIPPING

Kitchen scissors are convenient for snipping tender herbs like chives and chervil into attractive casual slivers.

SLIVERING

Tender herbs used for garnish — such as basil, mint and cilantro — are often more attractive when cut into chiffonade. Stack about 6 leaves on a cutting board and, if the leaves are large enough, roll them up. Using a sharp chef's knife or snippers, cut the roll crosswise into thin slivers.

CHOPPING

Pile herb leaves on a cutting board. Securing the tip of a sharp chef's knife with your free hand, use a rocking motion to chop herbs as finely as you wish. If you are chopping a large quantity of herbs, you can pulse them in a food processor. Make sure the blade is very sharp. For a small quantity of herbs, use a mini food processor rather than a large model.

USE QUICKLY

Once chopped, herbs quickly lose their flavor. Wait until just before using them to chop, tear or snip herbs. If you are entertaining and would like to get some of the preparation out of the way in advance, strip herb leaves from stems, wash and dry carefully. Enclose the leaves in a plastic food-storage bag and refrigerate until you are ready to chop.

PRESERVING HERBS

Whether you have a single pot of herbs on the deck or an extensive garden, access to homegrown herbs makes cooking a pleasure during the summer. But at the end of the growing season, you may want to capture the flavor of summer and prepare for winter cooking by preserving your herbs. Here's how.

HARVESTING

When preserving herbs, gather them when they are at their peak, just before they start to flower. Choose a sunny day and pick herbs midmorning after the dew has evaporated, but before the sun causes them to wilt. Discard any bruised or blemished leaves.

STOCKING UP ON HERB SAUCES

One of the most practical ways to preserve herbs is to make sauces and compound butters for the freezer. Make up a large batch of *Traditional Basil Pesto* (page 157) or *Parsley-Walnut Pesto* (page 162). Divide the pesto among containers and freeze for up to 6 months. Just thaw in the refrigerator and toss with pasta for a quick meal. Herb-flavored butters are another good option. You can use the recipe for *Shallot-Mustard Herb Butter* (page 163) or one of its variations as a guideline. Form butter into cylinders, wrap in plastic wrap and freeze for up to 6 months. Slice off pieces of butter as needed.

FREEZING

Tender leaf herbs, such as basil, chives, cilantro, dill, mint and parsley, are good candidates for freezing. There are a number of techniques for freezing herbs, but based on my testing, I have found that blanching herbs prior to freezing produces far superior results.

Freezing Herbs by Blanching Method. Trim stems from herb sprigs. Wash leaves. Bring a large saucepan of water to a boil. Place a bowl of ice water and a tray lined with a clean kitchen towel or paper towels beside the stove. Drop leaves *briefly* (just a few seconds) into the boiling water. With a slotted spoon,

transfer leaves to ice water to chill quickly, and then pat dry with towels. Spread herbs in a single layer on a wax paper-lined baking sheet and place in the freezer about 1 hour or until solid. Transfer to plastic food-storage bags; seal, label and freeze for up to 4 months. Frozen herbs are fine for flavoring, but are not suitable for garnishes. Chop frozen herbs with a knife or in your food processor.

Making Herb Ice Cubes. Place about 1 tablespoon chopped fresh herbs in each compartment of an ice cube tray. Add enough boiling water to cover herbs (boiling water replaces blanching) and freeze about 5 hours or until solid. Unmold ice cubes into a plastic food-storage bag and freeze for up to 4 months. This is the simplest method for freezing herbs. Herb ice cubes are handy for seasoning sauces and stews.

DRYING

This is the age-old method for preserving herbs. Sturdy herbs, such as rosemary, thyme, oregano and sage, are good candidates for drying. A food dehydrator, which provides uniform air circulation and controlled low heat, is the most efficient way to dry herbs, but they can also be simply hung to dry.

Drying Herbs in a Dehydrator. Wash and thoroughly dry herbs, then strip leaves from stems. Line dehydrator screens with cheesecloth so leaves won't fall through the screen. (Leaves will shrink as they dry.) Place herb leaves on screens and place trays in dehydrator.
Dehydrate at low (90°F) 12 to 24 hours or until herbs crumble easily between your fingertips. Unless herbs will be used in a mixture, such as *herbes de Provence*, dry only one kind of herb at a time to prevent flavors from mingling.

Drying Herbs by Hanging. Do not remove stems. Rinse herb sprigs and pat dry thoroughly. Tie small bunches together at stems. Punch holes in a brown paper bag with a hole punch or skewer. Place leafy ends in the prepared bag. (The bag will protect herbs from dust and minimize light.) Secure bag around stems with a string or elastic band. Hang bag, stem-ends up, in a well-ventilated place until leaves crumble easily between your fingers. This will take 5 to 10 days.

Herb Essentials **11**

Storing Dried Herbs. Trim stems, if necessary, and place herb leaves in a clean jar. Secure lid and store in a cupboard away from heat-producing appliances for up to 6 months. Just before using, crumble dried leaves with your fingertips to release their fragrance.

HERB-INFUSED VINEGAR

Herb-flavored vinegars allow you to enjoy the subtle flavor of herbs in your salads throughout the year. Herbs that complement salads — such as tarragon, burnet, dill, mint and basil — are good candidates for herb-infused vinegar.

Making Herb Vinegar. Wash and thoroughly dry 1 cup of herb sprigs, discarding any damaged leaves. Lightly bruise the herb sprigs to release their fragrance. (A mortar and pestle works well.) Place herbs in a sterilized wide-mouth 1-pint glass jar. In small saucepan, heat 2 cups white wine vinegar or rice vinegar until almost simmering. Pour vinegar over herbs. Cover and let steep overnight. Place a clean and dry herb sprig in a sterilized decorative bottle. Pour infused vinegar through a cheesecloth or coffee filter-lined funnel into the bottle. Cork or secure lid on the bottle and store vinegar in a cupboard away from heat-producing appliances. Use within 1 year.

Caution On Herb-Infused Oil. Despite serious health risks, I continue to see dangerous recipes for herb-infused oils in recently published cookbooks. This is disturbing because when executed incorrectly, the procedure of infusing herbs (and garlic and other aromatics) can lead to botulism, a serious and potentially fatal form of food poisoning. A container of oil is an anaerobic environment. When herbs (which are likely to have some soil contamination) are added, the result is an environment favorable to the growth of *botulinum* bacteria. Blanching herbs in boiling water does not kill the spores of *Clostridium botulinum*. However, acid does prevent the growth of these spores.

To make a safe infused oil, take the following precautions. Wash and dry herbs carefully. Be sure to add 1 tablespoon of an acidic ingredient, such as vinegar or lemon juice, at a ratio of 1 tablespoon per cup of oil. Store infusion in the refrigerator for no longer than 1 week.

CLASSIC HERB COMBOS

Here are some time-tested and classic ways to combine herbs.

BOUQUET GARNI

This herb bundle is used to flavor French-braised and long-simmered dishes. Tie the whole sprigs together securely so the bouquet can easily be removed before serving. Sprigs of parsley, thyme and bay leaf are standard. But a celery rib, leek leaf and strip of orange peel may also be included. To make a standard *bouquet garni*, gather together about 8 sprigs of fresh parsley, 8 sprigs of fresh or dried thyme and 1 bay leaf. Wrap butcher's twine up and down the length of the bundle and tie securely. Or enclose herbs in a double layer of cheesecloth and secure tightly with twine. When using *bouquet garni* ingredients to flavor stocks and other dishes that will be strained, don't bother to tie components together. If you will be using chopped parsley to finish the dish, reserve leaves for that purpose and make the *bouquet garni* with parsley stems only.

FINES HERBES

This French quartet includes chopped fresh parsley, tarragon, chervil and chives, combined in equal proportions. Only fresh herbs are used. A delicate mixture, you can use it in salads, egg dishes and light sauces. Always add *fines herbes* at the end of cooking.

HERBES DE PROVENCE

This popular mixture of dried herbs typifies the seasonings widely used in the south of France. It may include some or all of the following: rosemary, thyme, savory, sage, basil, marjoram, bay leaf, lavender and anise. The specific mix, however, may vary according to preferences of the cook. You can find commercial jars of *herbes de Provence* in specialty stores, but they are expensive and may not be as fresh as you would like. For the most flavorful blend, combine your own, preferably from home-dried herbs. I recommend staying with herbs that stand up well when dried.

Here's how to blend your own *herbes de Provence*. In a small jar with a tight-fitting lid, mix 1 tablespoon dried thyme, 1 tablespoon dried rosemary, 1 tablespoon dried oregano and 1 tablespoon dried savory. If desired, add a pinch of dried lavender and crushed anise seed. If you have a quantity of these dried herbs you would like to preserve for winter and plan to use the mixture within 6 months, follow the basic proportions and make a larger batch.

GREMOLADA

A simple mixture of parsley, lemon peel and garlic, gremolada is used in Italian cooking, most notably as a garnish for the famous Milanese dish, *osso bucco* (braised veal shanks). It is also a delicious way to finish lamb, seafood, vegetable stew or seafood risotto. The fresh-tasting parsley and lemon rind counter the garlic's pungency. For a good balance, use a ratio of 1/3 cup chopped fresh parsley, 1 teaspoon freshly grated lemon peel and 2 medium minced garlic cloves. Just toss the mixture together shortly before using, and sprinkle over hot dishes; heat releases the fragrance.

PERSILLADE

In France, chopped fresh parsley flavored with minced garlic is known as persillade. It is stirred into quick sautés of meat, fish or vegetables at the last minute.

ZATAR

This blend from the Middle East is often served with flatbreads. Zatar is the Arabic word for wild thyme. To make a zatar herb blend, grind 2 tablespoons dried thyme, 2 tablespoons toasted sesame seeds and 1/4 teaspoon salt in a spice grinder. Transfer to a small bowl or jar and stir in 1/2 teaspoon ground sumac. Sumac, a spice with a slightly tart flavor, is made from dried berries of the sumac bush. You can find it in Middle Eastern markets. Store zatar, tightly covered, in the refrigerator for several months. Mix with a little extra-virgin olive oil and serve as a dip for warm pita breads.

HERB GARNISHES

Herbs are the quintessential garnish. You just cannot go wrong embellishing a plate with sprigs of an herb featured in the dish. But in addition to the straight-forward herb sprig or sprinkle of slivered herbs, there are some fun and interesting ways to garnish with herbs.

CHIVE "RIBBONS"

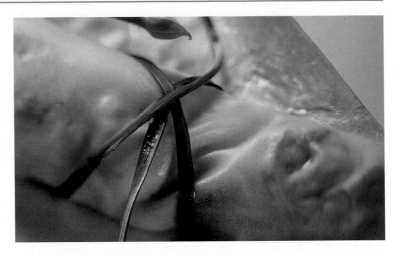

A long chive ribbon is an attractive way to secure and decorate a bouquet of herb sprigs, bundle of vegetables, spring roll or beggar's purse (an appetizer made by enclosing a spoonful of caviar and a dollop of *crème fraîche* in a crepe wrapper). To make chives pliable enough to tie, blanch them in boiling water for a few seconds, then place in a bowl of ice water and pat dry.

HERB BOUQUETS

A bouquet of assorted herb sprigs is an appealing way to garnish an appetizer tray or roast turkey. Sage, rosemary, thyme and bay leaves make an attractive grouping. Tie stems together loosely with a chive ribbon and place them on the platter.

FRIED PARSLEY

This is a classic garnish for fried fish and other fried foods. In this case, curly parsley is a better choice than Italian parsley. To prepare fried parsley, trim sprigs, leaving about 1 inch of stem. Wash parsley and dry thoroughly. (Just a little moisture will cause the oil to splatter.) Place about 1 inch vegetable or olive oil in a deep fryer or heavy saucepan; heat to 375°F. Carefully drop a handful of parsley sprigs into the hot oil and turn with a skimmer. Fry 10 to 15 seconds or until crisp but not colored. Lift sprigs out with skimmer and drain on a paper towel. Sprinkle lightly with salt and serve immediately.

FROSTED HERB SPRIGS

Herb sprigs coated with glistening sugar make interesting and attractive garnishes for desserts and pastries. Herbs with stubby, thick leaves (such as rosemary, lemon verbena and lemon thyme) work best. Frosted rosemary sprigs, accompanied by frosted cranberries, are festive-looking and are a lovely way to decorate a *bûche de Noël* (Yule log) or holiday cheesecake. To frost herbs, rinse sprigs and dry thoroughly. In small bowl, stir 1 pasteurized egg white briskly with a fork. Set a bowl of superfine sugar beside it. Place a wire rack over a sheet of parchment paper or a baking sheet. Holding on to the stem, dip an herb sprig into the egg white and shake off the excess. Dip into sugar, turn to coat, and sprinkle again with sugar. Place on rack and let dry 1½ to 2 hours.

Note that because of food safety, use only pasteurized egg whites. You can find pasteurized dried egg whites, such as Just Whites, and refrigerated pasteurized liquid egg whites, such as All Whites, in most supermarkets.

EDIBLE FLOWERS

A few herbs, such as chives and borage, produce edible flowers that make great garnishes for salads. Nasturtium flowers have a delightful peppery taste that is welcome in salads. For sweet dishes, pansies, violas and rose petals make lovely decorative finishes. Be sure to avoid any flowers that may have been sprayed with pesticides.

TIPS FOR COOKING WITH HERBS

Here are a couple of tips for cooking creatively — and deliciously — with herbs.

Timing. As a general rule, dried herbs and sturdy fresh herbs, such as rosemary, thyme, oregano and bay leaf, are added at the beginning of cooking. Delicate herbs, such as parsley, basil, dill, cilantro and tarragon, should be used as seasonings at the end of cooking.

Herb Infusions. A subtle infusion of herbs is effective in both savory and sweet dishes.

The infusion technique is useful when you are making soups. Simmering canned broth with rosemary sprigs and garlic for about 20 minutes is a great trick for adding depth of flavor to a canned product. A tea infuser is handy for containing the flavorings because it can be simply lifted out when the infusion is ready. (Or broth can be passed through a strainer.)

A subtle herbal infusion gives a magical quality to fruit desserts. To infuse milk for a custard or sugar syrup for a fruit salad or sorbet, add herb sprigs to the hot liquid and let it steep for about 30 minutes, then strain out the herbs.

To release maximum fragrance, lightly bruise the herbs before infusing them in vinegar or cold fruit juice. To bruise: Place herb sprigs in a medium bowl. Using a wooden mortar or large wooden spoon, crush herbs until you notice the fragrance.

GRILLING WITH HERBS

Herbs add life and flavor to your grilling creations. Here are some ideas.

Add Aroma to the Fire. If you have an abundant supply of herbs, toss a few sprigs of a sturdy herb (such as rosemary, thyme or bay leaf) that complements the food you are grilling onto the coals or grid over a gas flame.

Herbal Protection. Use herbs to protect meat, chicken or fish from the grill's searing heat. Lightly oil food, then stick whole sage or mint leaves onto meat surfaces before placing on the grill. The herbs will also impart a subtle flavor.

Creative Kabobs. Thread whole sage leaves or bay leaves (soaked in water, if dried) between pieces of food when assembling skewers.

Lemongrass Skewers. Edible skewers made from lemongrass stalks add an extra dimension and interesting presentation to Southeast Asian-flavored kabobs. To prepare a stalk of lemongrass for use as a skewer, trim the stem end and enough of the leafy end so the stalk is about 10 inches long. Remove outer leaves so the stalk is between 1/4- and 1/2- inch thick. Using a small and sharp knife, whittle the stem end into a sharp point. Wrap the stalk in plastic wrap and freeze 1 hour or until firm. When you are ready to assemble kabobs, first use a metal skewer to pierce a hole through the food, then thread onto lemongrass skewers.

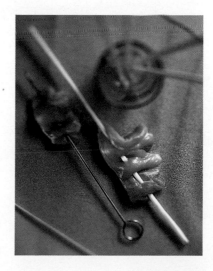

HERB GLOSSARY

Herb or spice? Dried herbs and spices share space on the spice racks of North American kitchens. But few cooks know the subtle distinctions between these two flavoring agents.

"Herb" generally refers to a plant from which the fragrant leafy parts (and sometimes stems) are used for culinary, cosmetic or medicinal purposes. Most herbs can be cultivated in temperate zones and typically do not have woody stems. Fresh herbs are often preferred, but sturdier ones can be dried for longer storage. "Spices," on the other hand, come from the seeds, roots and barks of plants. Most spices (but not all) come from tropical regions. They are generally used in dried form.

Although there are countless plants that may meet the botanical definition of an herb, the focus in this book is herbs for culinary purposes. The following is a guide to 25 of the most useful kitchen herbs.

ANGELICA

DESCRIPTION

With a taste and fragrance as delicate and lovely as its name, angelica is an uncommon herb that is definitely worth seeking out. A member of the parsley family, this herb resembles celery — but it is much larger. At maturity, angelica can reach a towering height of 6 feet. It is native to Europe and Asia but is easily cultivated in North America. Angelica is generally considered a biennial. Its distinctive flavor is reminiscent of licorice, vanilla and celery.

TRADITIONAL USES

Although you may not be aware of it, you may be familiar with the taste of angelica if you enjoy herb liqueurs. The roots and seeds contribute a delicate flavor to Benedictine and Chartreuse, while the roots are used to flavor gin. Perhaps angelica is best known for its stems, which are traditionally candied. European pastry chefs use candied angelica to decorate cakes, pastries and puddings. Angelica has a long-term relationship with rhubarb. It mellows the tartness and astringency, and contributes a delicate herbal fragrance to rhubarb dishes. Cooking rhubarb with angelica allows you to reduce sugar slightly.

PREPARATION AND COOKING TIPS

The stems are the most useful part in cooking. Add a few tablespoons of finely diced angelica stems to a rhubarb pie or compote (see *Rhubarb Fool*, page 148).

STORAGE

Enclose stalks in a plastic food-storage bag and refrigerate up to 4 days. The traditional method of preserving angelica is to candy the stems in sugar syrup. This somewhat complicated process involves first blanching angelica and then submerging and boiling repeatedly in sugar syrup of specific densities, and finally, drying.

COMPLEMENTS

Angelica works well with rhubarb and other tart fruits such as gooseberries or damsen plums.

GROWING ANGELICA

Angelica archangelica

Plant type—Biennial or short-lived perennial.

Size—4 to 8 feet tall, 3 feet wide.

Light—Light shade.

Soil—Humus-rich, moist.

Propagation—Sow fresh seed outdoors in early autumn. Keep moist but do not cover, as seed requires light to germinate. Seed loses viability in 3 months, but it will keep up to a year if refrigerated in an airtight container. Thin to 3 feet apart. If seeds are not sown in place in the garden the previous autumn, transplant to the permanent site in mid-spring.

Care—Remove flowers as they develop to prolong the life of the plant. Let flowers develop on at least one plant to provide seed for new plants. Spray aphids or spider mites with horticultural soap.

BASIL

DESCRIPTION

Although supermarkets now stock this leafy herb year-round, fragrant basil epitomizes the sweet taste of summer. Basil is native to India, Africa and Asia but has been long valued as a culinary herb in Mediterranean regions. The flavor is sweet, with a hint of pepper and undertones of mint and cloves.

VARIETIES

In addition to common sweet basil, there are numerous varieties to explore. Here are a few interesting options: Bush basil is a dwarf variety with tiny leaves. Opal basil and purple ruffles basil have attractive dark maroon-colored leaves and look stunning in an herb vinegar. Thai basil offers distinctive anise tones and is appropriate for Thai and Vietnamese dishes. Cinnamon basil and lemon basil offer slight variations on the basil theme.

TRADITIONAL USES

Basil is a fine salad herb and has a much-appreciated affinity with tomatoes. Basil, of course, is the dominant flavoring in the classic Italian sauce, pesto. In Asia, basil flavors curries and adds life to salads and soups.

PREPARATION AND COOKING TIPS

Fresh is best; dried basil just doesn't compare. To preserve the flavor of basil, use it raw or add it to a dish at the end of cooking. Because basil tends to turn black when bruised, tear leaves into smaller pieces before adding to a rustic salad or sauce, or use a sharp knife to cut leaves into chiffonade (page 9). Scatter torn basil leaves over fresh tomato salads, stir into tomato sauce or finish a vegetable sauté or soup with slivered basil. Add torn leaves to green salads and layer in sandwiches instead of lettuce. Basil is also good in sweet dishes.

STORAGE

Because the recommended temperature for holding basil is 48° to 50°F (colder than room temperature, warmer than a refrigerator), storing basil is difficult. It turns black when subjected to temperatures below 48°F and wilts quickly at warmer temperatures. So purchase or harvest basil the day you plan to use it. If you are a gardener or frequent farmers' markets, you will certainly want to preserve some of the late-summer abundance for winter. One of the best ways to do this is to make a large batch of pesto and freeze in small containers for up to 6 months. You can also freeze basil. For best results and optimum flavor, blanch it as directed on page 10.

COMPLEMENTS

Use basil with garlic, tomatoes and other summer vegetables such as zucchini, bell peppers, eggplant and corn.

GROWING BASIL

Ocimum basilicum

Plant type—Tender annual.

Size—1 to 3 feet tall, 1 to 2 feet wide.

Light—Full sun.

Soil—Humus-rich, moist, well-drained.

Propagation—Start seed indoors 4 weeks before the last frost, planting ⅛-inch deep and with 75°F bottom heat; germination takes about 3 days. Set out when all danger of frost is past and night temperatures are above 65°F. Seed can also be sown directly into the garden at this time. Space plants 12 to 18 inches apart. The basils easily adapt to containers filled with a fast-draining potting mix. Feed monthly with a balanced fertilizer according to the manufacturer's directions.

Care—Fertilize at 6-week intervals during the growing season with a balanced organic fertilizer. Remove the flower spikes as they emerge to keep the plant bushy and producing new leaves.

BAY LEAF

DESCRIPTION

One of the most indispensable herbs in European and North American cooking, bay leaves slowly release their pungent, somewhat piney aroma to numerous soups and stews. This herb is also known as bay laurel, laurel leaf or sweet bay. It comes from a perennial evergreen shrub that thrives in the Mediterranean region, although it can be grown in North America. In colder areas, it survives best in a container that can be brought indoors for the winter. Dried bay leaves are essential seasonings in any pantry. Some supermarkets now sell fresh bay leaves. These are shinier and a deeper green than the familiar dried leaves.

VARIETIES

Of the two main varieties, Turkish bay and California bay, the more subtly flavored Turkish leaves are preferred for cooking.

TRADITIONAL USES

Along with parsley and thyme, bay leaf is a key ingredient in the *bouquet garni* used to flavor classic French stocks and braises. Bay leaves are routinely added to meat dishes, cream sauces, potatoes and rice pilafs for a subtle infusion of fragrance during cooking.

PREPARATION AND COOKING

Keep fresh or dried leaves whole and always remove them from the dish before serving to avoid any possibility of choking. Don't overdo it with bay — too much will make a dish bitter. One leaf is generally enough to flavor a dish for 4 to 6 people. In addition to stews, stocks, pilafs and sauces, bay will perk up your cooking in a variety of ways: For example, drop a leaf into the water used for boiling seafood or potatoes. You can also thread bay leaves between chunks of meat, poultry or seafood to make attractive and flavorful kabobs (see *Swordfish Souvlaki*, page 130). Try flavoring desserts with fresh bay leaves; you can infuse the milk for sweet custards or sugar syrup for poaching fruit with subtle scent of bay.

STORAGE

Store fresh bay leaves in a plastic food-storage bag in the refrigerator. They will keep for several days. Remember that dried bay leaves lose their fragrance over time. Try to use within 6 months.

COMPLEMENTS

Bay works well with strong flavors like meat, poultry and seafood, but also enhances delicate cream sauces.

GROWING BAY
Laurus nobilis

Plant type—Woody, evergreen shrub or tree.

Size—Up to 50 feet when grown year-round outdoors; 5 to 10 feet in containers.

Light—Full sun to light shade.

Soil—Humus-rich, well-drained.

Propagation—Difficult to start from seed, but if you're feeling adventurous, try them indoors with 75°F bottom heat; germination takes 4 weeks. Cuttings are much more reliable, but still a slow process. Take cuttings in the fall from young shoots; rooting may take 6 to 9 months.

Care—Except where hardy, grow bay in containers filled with a fast-draining potting mix and overwinter indoors. Fertilize in the spring with a balanced fertilizer according to the manufacturer's directions. Pinch out tip growth to encourage branching. Bay is very susceptible to scale. Control with sprays of horticultural soap or a summer horticultural oil.

URNET

DESCRIPTION

This hardy perennial was commonly used by Europeans as far back as the 15th century. Sadly, this old-fashioned herb is seldom used in contemporary cooking. Native to Europe, it is also known as salad burnet. It has very pretty fern-like foliage, and the delicate leaves have a refreshing cucumber-like flavor. If you would like to brighten your salads with burnet, you will probably have to grow your own. In mild climates, it may stay green year-round.

TRADITIONAL USES

Burnet has long been enjoyed in salads and is used to flavor wine and beverages.

PREPARATION AND COOKING TIPS

Use only tender young leaves, as old ones may be tough and bitter. Rinse sprigs and pat dry. Strip leaves from stems; leave whole or chop. Add whole burnet leaves to salad greens. Flavor cream cheese spreads and yogurt (or sour-cream) dips with chopped burnet. Use whole leaves to garnish cold soups and sprigs in wine coolers.

STORAGE

This is an herb to enjoy fresh from the garden. It loses its cucumber flavor when dried. To preserve the delicate taste of burnet for the winter, use it in an herb vinegar (page 12).

GROWING BURNET

Sanguisorba officinalis

Plant type—Herbaceous perennial.

Size—2 to 4 feet tall, 2 feet wide.

Light—Full sun.

Soil—Moist, well-drained soil.

Propagation—Propagate by seed or by dividing established clumps. Sow seeds in March and thin out to 9 inches apart. You can also propagate by dividing roots in autumn so that they become well-established before the next summer's dry weather sets in.

Care—Pick off the flowers when they appear; you use only the stem and leaves of the herb. Burnet was originally used medicinally to help stop bleeding.

COMPLEMENTS

Burnet goes well with salad greens, fresh cheeses, yogurt and sour cream.

SAVORY

DESCRIPTION

With a flavor reminiscent of peppery thyme, savory is a highly useful and versatile herb. It has been valued as a seasoning since ancient times, and it deserves more prominence in contemporary North American cooking. Savory is a member of the mint family and is native to the Mediterranean.

VARIETIES

The important distinction is between summer savory, an annual, and winter savory, a shrubby perennial. Summer savory is generally preferred for cooking because the flavor is more delicate. Winter savory has a stronger, more pine-like flavor. It has a bushy appearance, and its leaves are more needlelike and dense than summer savory.

TRADITIONAL USES

The German name for savory is *bohnenkraut*, which translates as "bean herb." It enhances bean and legume dishes and is believed to have carminative (antiflatulent) properties. In northern Europe, savory is used in sausages. The French seasoning mixture, *herbes de Provence* (page 14), generally includes savory.

PREPARATION AND COOKING TIPS

Both winter and summer savory have a strong peppery flavor; use in small quantities. Rinse sprigs and pat dry. Chop and add to salads or sprinkle over cooked vegetable dishes. When simmering beans or lentils, tie several sprigs together with kitchen twine and add cooking liquid; retrieve the bundle before serving. If you are cutting back on salt, try compensating by adding a pinch of savory to soups, salads, vegetables and meat dishes. Dried savory can be used in long-simmered dishes.

STORAGE

Enclose sprigs in a plastic food-storage bag and refrigerate up to 4 days. Savory is suitable for drying.

COMPLEMENTS

Savory enhances green beans, dried beans, lentils, split peas, meat, poultry and strongly flavored vegetables such as Brussels sprouts and cabbage.

GROWING SAVORY

Satureja species

Plant type—Summer savory is an annual. Winter savory is a woody, semi-evergreen perennial.

Size—Winter savory grows to 1 foot tall and as wide. Summer savory grows to 18 inches tall and 1 foot wide.

Light—Full sun.

Soil—Well-drained soil. Summer savory needs soil that is more moist.

Propagation—Start seeds of summer savory six weeks before the last frost and transplant outdoors after all danger of frost is past. Or sow directly into the garden about a week before the last frost. Space 6 inches apart. Savory seeds germinate more quickly if soaked overnight in hot water before planting.

Care—Summer savory needs good air circulation around it to prevent fungal diseases. To limit its sprawling tendencies, mound soil around the base of the stems. Both summer and winter savory adapt well to containers filled with fast-draining potting soil and a monthly feeding. Both kinds may be brought indoors during the winter.

HISO

DESCRIPTION

Sushi fans may be familiar with the aromatic herb, shiso, which is used primarily in Japanese cooking. The English name is perilla. Shiso, an annual, belongs to the same family as mint and basil. It is native to Asia, but is also cultivated in Europe and North America. Graceful in appearance, shiso leaves are large (2 to 3 inches wide) and have attractive jagged edges. The flavor of shiso is fresh and delicate with a hint of cumin. You can find fresh shiso leaves in Japanese markets. Since shiso can be difficult to find, it may be worth growing your own.

Green Shiso

VARIETIES

Green shiso is the most common, but you can also find red (or purple) shiso. The red variety is sometimes called beefsteak plant. It provides color for the Japanese pickled plums known as *umeboshi*.

GROWING SHISO
Perilla frutescens

Plant type—Annual.

Size—3 feet tall, 1 foot wide.

Light—Full sun.

Soil—Moist but well-drained soil. Extra organic matter in the soil is beneficial.

Propagation—Propagate by seed. Direct seed in good soil in midspring. Shiso germinates in about 11 days and grows rapidly. It has many medicinal uses such as treating fever, headache, nasal congestion and cough. It has antiseptic properties and also helps alleviate seafood poisoning. Shiso is extensively cultivated in Asia.

Care—Shiso self-seeds in most gardens, and some gardeners consider it a bit pesky.

TRADITIONAL USES

Chopped shiso is used in sushi, salads, rice and noodle dishes. Leaves are dipped in batter and deep-fried as tempura.

PREPARATION AND COOKING TIPS

Rinse leaves and pat dry. Stack, then cut into thin slivers or chop. Stir chopped shiso into rice or sprinkle slivered shiso over salads with Japanese flavors. Use the pretty whole leaves as a garnish or as an attractive bed for a salad.

STORAGE

Enclose shiso in a plastic food-storage bag and refrigerate up to 4 days.

Red Shiso

COMPLEMENTS

Use shiso in dishes with fish and seafood, soba noodles and rice.

SORREL

DESCRIPTION

Sorrel is considered both an herb and a vegetable. It is distinguished by its tangy, sour flavor, a characteristic highly appreciated by the French. The tartness is due to the presence of oxalic acid (also found in spinach and rhubarb). Sorrel is a hardy perennial with green leaves that resemble small spinach leaves. It is also known as dock and sour grass. You can sometimes find sorrel in specialty produce markets. But if you are a fan of this puckery plant, you will probably want to ensure a supply by growing it in your garden.

VARIETIES

Garden sorrel and true French sorrel are the varieties most commonly used in cooking. The two types are differentiated by the shape of their leaves. Garden sorrel has long and narrow leaves; true French sorrel has smaller, rounded leaves. True French sorrel is slightly less acidic and favored by some cooks.

TRADITIONAL USES

The best-known sorrel preparation is the French *potage Germiny*, a rich soup made from sorrel, broth, cream and egg yolks. Also in French cooking, a sauce of pureed sorrel, fish stock and butter is a classic pairing with fish.

PREPARATION AND COOKING TIPS

Trim stems and wash sorrel leaves as you would spinach. You can use a few torn *young* leaves to enliven a green salad. To make a chiffonade of sorrel, stack leaves and roll up. Use a chef's knife to cut the roll crosswise into thin strips. Sorrel cooks quickly, so add it toward the end of cooking. Sorrel also melts down into a puree easily. Just cook shredded sorrel in a little butter until it forms a puree. Finish the puree with cream or butter and use a sauce for fish. You can give sautéed spinach or Swiss chard an interesting tang with the addition of some shredded sorrel. Try sorrel in an omelet filling; sprinkle shredded sorrel over the egg mixture before folding the omelet.

GROWING SORREL

Rumex species

Plant type—Perennial.

Size—*R. acetosa* grows 6 inches tall, forming a ground-hugging mat, then reaches 18 inches when in bloom. Spreads rapidly.

Light—Full sun to light shade.

Soil—Humus-rich, moist, well-drained.

Propagation—Sow seed in spring directly into the garden several weeks before the last spring frost. Germination takes about a week. Space plants 1 foot apart. Divide in autumn at least every three years to help maintain vigorous plantings.

Care—Protect sorrel from slugs with traps or barriers. Choose a site carefully so that sorrel's invasive tendencies are not a problem. Growing sorrel in containers is a good way to limit its spreading ways. Use a fast-draining potting mix and a monthly feeding during the growing season with a balanced fertilizer. Overwinter in a protected place with mulch around the pot.

STORAGE

Wrap in paper towel and enclose in a plastic food-storage bag. Store in the refrigerator up to 4 days. For long-term storage, make sorrel puree and freeze up to 6 months.

COMPLEMENTS

Fish, eggs, potatoes and tender greens, such as spinach and Swiss chard, are enhanced by sorrel.

TARRAGON

DESCRIPTION

One of the most prized culinary herbs, tarragon plays a prominent role in some of the best-known classical French dishes. The delicate, bittersweet flavor has a suggestion of anise. This hardy perennial has slender, dark green leaves. It is believed that tarragon originated in Siberia and southern Russia, but it is now widely cultivated in Europe and North America.

VARIETIES

Of the two types of tarragon, French and Russian, French is the kind you want for cooking. It has the best flavor but cannot be reliably grown from seed. Russian tarragon, which is easier to grow, has little flavor. When purchasing a plant, check the label to be sure it is indeed French tarragon and make sure it has a distinctive tarragon aroma. Sweet marigold (also known as Mexican tarragon) has a flavor similar to tarragon but is actually a member of the marigold family. It is a good option for gardeners who live in hot climates where French tarragon does not thrive.

TRADITIONAL USES

Tarragon is one of the herbs used in the French herb mixture *fines herbes* (page 13). It is an essential seasoning in béarnaise sauce and is featured in the classic French dish, chicken with tarragon. In addition, it is commonly used to infuse a subtle flavor in vinegar.

PREPARATION AND COOKING TIPS

Rinse sprigs and pat dry. Strip leaves from stems and chop. The flavor of tarragon does not withstand heat, so add chopped tarragon at the end of cooking, or use in uncooked dishes. The charm of tarragon lies in its delicacy; use sparingly. Dried tarragon is not as flavorful as fresh but is a reasonable substitute in a pinch. Some ideas for using tarragon in your cooking: Sprinkle it over soft-boiled eggs or stir it into scrambled eggs. Flavor dressings for chicken salad or egg salad with tarragon. Add torn tarragon leaves to green salads.

STORAGE

Enclose tarragon sprigs in a plastic food-storage bag and refrigerate up to 2 days. To preserve the summery taste of tarragon for winter, make tarragon vinegar (page 12). Alternatively, make a batch of tarragon butter (see NOTES, page 163) for the freezer.

COMPLEMENTS

Tarragon pairs well with mustard, lemon, eggs, chicken and mild white fish such as sole or halibut.

GROWING TARRAGON

Artemisia dracunculus

Plant type—Perennial.

Size—2 feet tall, 2 feet wide.

Light—Full sun to light shade.

Soil—Humus-rich, well-drained.

Propagation—French tarragon cannot be started from seed. Divide in early spring. Take cuttings in midsummer. Space plants 2 feet apart.

Care—Pinch out the growing tips several times during the growing season. French tarragon needs well-drained soil. To maintain vigor, divide plants every 2 or 3 years. Provide a winter mulch or grow tarragon as an annual. French tarragon grows well in a container filled with a fast-draining potting mix and a monthly feeding with a balanced fertilizer. If brought indoors during the winter, it needs very bright light. To overwinter outdoors, put in a protected spot and surround the plant and pot with mulch.

HYME

DESCRIPTION

Thyme seems to work its magic behind the scenes. It doesn't make a splash like some of the livelier herbs, such as cilantro and dill. Yet it is one of the most useful and versatile herbs in the kitchen. Thyme has a warm, rich aroma with subtle pine undertones. It is a low-growing perennial shrub native to the western Mediterranean, and is a member of the mint family.

VARIETIES

There are numerous species of thyme. The type most widely used in cooking is common thyme. Within this group there is a popular variety called English thyme and also a variety called French thyme. Both varieties of common thyme are suitable for most recipes calling for thyme. In addition to the common variety, there are a number of flavored thymes that are of special interest to the cook. Lemon thyme has a delightful aroma, which complements light fish dishes, vegetables and fruits. Caraway thyme has a spicy fragrance that pairs well with red meats.

TRADITIONAL USES

Thyme is a component of *bouquet garni* (page 13), an essential flavoring in a large variety of French braised dishes, casseroles, soups, sauces and stocks. It is also typical in *herbes de Provence* (page 14). The Middle Eastern herb-spice blend called zatar (page 15) features thyme.

PREPARATION AND COOKING TIPS

Rinse sprigs and pat dry. Tie sprigs into a *bouquet garni* and add to long-simmered dishes; retrieve bouquet before serving. For chopped thyme, strip leaves from stems and chop. Thyme retains flavor well and is generally added at the beginning of cooking. Dried thyme is a reasonable alternative to fresh. Use 3 parts fresh thyme to 1 part dried thyme. Add several sprigs of fresh thyme or a generous pinch of dried whenever you are making a hearty soup, meat stew or bean dish. Toss root vegetables with chopped fresh or dried thyme before roasting. For a simple appetizer, marinate olives in thyme and lemon juice.

STORAGE

Enclose fresh thyme sprigs in a plastic food-storage bag and refrigerate up to 1 week. To preserve thyme, either hang to dry or use a dehydrator (page 11).

COMPLEMENTS

Red meat, pork, chicken, turkey, winter vegetables (such as squash, parsnips and celeriac), lentils, beans, apples and pears work well with thyme.

GROWING THYME

Thymus species

Plant type—Evergreen to semi-evergreen woody perennial. Hardiness varies, depending on the species and cultivar.

Size—Common thyme and lemon thyme grow to 12 inches tall. Broad-leaved thyme grows to 8 inches tall. Creeping thyme, caraway thyme and mother-of-thyme grow 2 to 3 inches tall.

Light—Full sun to light shade.

Soil—Well-drained.

Propagation—Start seed indoors 6 to 8 weeks before the last frost in spring. Germination is best at 70°F and takes about a week. Space plants 1 foot apart. Divide or take cuttings in spring. Thymes fill a container and cascade over the edges beautifully. Use a fast-draining potting mix and feed monthly with a balanced fertilizer.

Care—Trim plants in early spring to remove any dead growth and to encourage new branches. Trim again after flowering.

ABOUT GARLIC

Although it's not a true herb, one cannot underestimate the importance of garlic in cooking. Here are some ins and outs of using garlic. Distinguished by its notorious pungency, garlic is one of the key seasonings in Mediterranean and Asian cuisines. It is the most strongly flavored member of the onion (*allium*) family. Its potency varies depending on age and variety. The flavor is most delicate at the beginning of the season in late spring and early summer. The color of garlic ranges from white to burgundy. The giant elephant garlic has a much milder flavor than standard-sized bulbs. To help you get the most out of garlic, here are some tips for using it:

To Peel and Crush Garlic: Separate a clove from the bulb and place it on a cutting board. Set the flat side of a chef's knife over the garlic and pound knife gently with your fist. The skin should separate from the flesh; discard skin. If you are peeling a lot of garlic, before peeling, soak cloves in water for 15 to 30 minutes to loosen skin and reduce stickiness.

To Mince Garlic: Hold the side of chef's knife over a garlic clove, pound knife again to crush the clove further. If using garlic raw, remove the dark green germ if there is any. (The germ can be bitter.) Holding the knife at an angle, use an up-and-down motion to mince garlic finely. Minced garlic can be used in cooked dishes, marinades, and sparingly in salads.

To Mash Garlic with Salt: Place crushed, peeled garlic in a mortar and pestle, and sprinkle with salt. Mash into a paste with the pestle. (If you do not have a mortar and pestle, leave garlic on cutting board, sprinkle with salt and use side of chef's knife to mash.) Mashed garlic is preferred in salads and sauces that will not be cooked because it has a mellower flavor than coarsely chopped garlic or garlic that has been crushed in a garlic press.

To Roast Garlic: Peel away the papery outer layer and slice the tip off a garlic bulb to expose cloves. Place on a square of aluminum foil, sprinkle with 1 tablespoon olive oil or water. Pinch edges of foil together to seal packet. Bake at 400°F for about 45 minutes or until garlic flesh is soft. Let cool slightly and then squeeze the soft garlic into a bowl. Use roasted garlic to enrich mashed potatoes and salad dressings or to spread over country bread.

For a Delicate Touch with Garlic: Just rub the cut side of a garlic clove over a salad bowl or baking dish.

When Cooking Minced Garlic: Take care not to let it burn because it will become bitter.

GROWING GARLIC
Allium Sativum

Plant type—Perennial bulb.

Size—2 feet tall, 8 inches wide.

Light—Full sun.

Soil—Humus-rich, moist, well-drained.

Propagation—Although you can start garlic from seed, it is much easier to plant individual cloves. Plant the cloves 2 inches deep and 4 inches apart, 4 to 6 weeks before the first frost in autumn. Use only the larger cloves. The smaller ones can be eaten or planted in a separate area, spacing 2 inches apart for spring baby garlic (which is eaten like scallions). Plant in rows or plant groups of six or eight bulbs. Garlic is a good companion plant for roses, cabbage, eggplant, tomatoes and fruit trees.

Care—Apply several inches of mulch in late autumn. Remove the flower stalks in spring or early summer so that all the plant's energy goes into the developing bulb.

RECIPE POTPOURRI

What better way to start a meal than with an herb-flecked appetizer or a fragrant herb bread? A veritable potpourri of little meals, this chapter features an eclectic selection of breakfast and brunch dishes, snacks, appetizers, breads and pizzas.

Carmelized Red Onion, Olive
and Goat Cheese Galette, page 64

SMOKED SALMON CANAPES

These simple, crowd-pleasing appetizers feature the time-honored combination of salmon and dill. Vodka provides an appetite-teasing kick, but if you prefer to avoid alcohol, substitute brewed black tea.

2	tablespoons fresh lemon juice
2	tablespoons vodka, if desired
1	tablespoon extra-virgin olive oil
2	teaspoons Dijon mustard
1/4	teaspoon freshly ground pepper
8	oz. sliced smoked salmon, finely chopped
1/4	cup finely diced red onion
3	tablespoons chopped fresh dill
2	tablespoons drained capers, coarsely chopped
24	slices baguette (1/4 inch)
24	fresh dill sprigs

❶ In medium bowl, combine lemon juice, vodka, oil, mustard and pepper; blend with wire whisk. Add salmon, onion, chopped dill and capers; toss to mix well. *(Topping can be prepared up to 8 hours ahead. Cover and refrigerate.)*

❷ Heat oven to 325°F. Spray baking sheet with nonstick cooking spray. Arrange baguette slices in single layer on baking sheet. Spray tops of slices lightly with nonstick cooking spray.

❸ Bake baguette slices 15 to 20 minutes or just until crisp and very light golden. *(Toasts can be prepared up to 8 hours ahead. Store in airtight container at room temperature.)*

❹ Just before serving, mound about 1 tablespoon topping on each slice of toast. Garnish each with 1 dill sprig.

24 appetizers.

Preparation time: 15 minutes. Ready to serve: 30 minutes.

Per appetizer: 30 calories, 1.5 g total fat (0.5 g saturated fat), 0 mg cholesterol, 120 mg sodium, 0 g fiber.

CARAMELIZED RED ONION, OLIVE AND GOAT CHEESE GALETTE

This savory tart is great for parties and potlucks. It is based on the Provençal specialty, pissaladière, which plays the sweetness of caramelized onions against savory ripe olives and fragrant herbs.

CRUST
2 cups all-purpose flour
1/4 cup (1 oz.) freshly grated Parmesan cheese
2 teaspoons baking powder
1/2 teaspoon salt
3/4 cup reduced-fat cottage cheese
1/3 cup reduced-fat milk
1/4 cup olive oil
1 1/2 teaspoons sugar

TOPPING
3 teaspoons olive oil
6 cups thinly sliced red onions
1 teaspoon salt
1 tablespoon balsamic vinegar
2 garlic cloves, minced
1 cup (4 oz.) creamy goat cheese, crumbled
1/2 cup pitted kalamata olives, quartered
2 teaspoons each chopped fresh thyme, rosemary
1/2 teaspoon freshly ground pepper

❶ In medium bowl, combine flour, Parmesan cheese, baking powder and 1/2 teaspoon salt; mix well. In food processor, puree cottage cheese until smooth. Add milk, oil and sugar; process until smooth. Add flour mixture; pulse 4 to 5 times or just until dough begins to form.

❷ On lightly floured surface, knead dough several times; do not overwork. Press dough into flattened round; dust with flour. Wrap in plastic wrap; refrigerate while preparing filling. *(Dough can be prepared up to 2 days ahead. Cover and refrigerate.)* In large skillet, heat 1 teaspoon of the oil over medium heat until hot. Add onions and salt; cook 10 to 15 minutes or until very tender and lightly caramelized, stirring frequently. (If onions start to scorch, add a few tablespoons of water.) Add vinegar and garlic; cook and stir 1 minute. Remove from heat; cool. *(Onions can be prepared up to 2 days ahead. Cover and refrigerate.)*

❸ Heat oven to 400°F. Spray 15x10x1-inch pan with nonstick cooking spray. On lightly floured surface, roll dough to form 15 1/2x10 1/2-inch rectangle. Place dough in pan, folding in edges as necessary. Press edges with fork to flute. Spread onion filling over dough. Scatter goat cheese and olives over filling. Sprinkle with thyme, rosemary and pepper. Drizzle with remaining 2 teaspoons oil.

❹ Bake 20 to 30 minutes or until crust is golden brown and firm. Cool in pan on wire rack 5 minutes. (Galette can be made up to 1 day ahead; cool completely. Cover and refrigerate. To reheat, cover loosely with foil; bake at 325°F 10 to 15 minutes.) Slide galette onto cutting board. With pizza cutter or knife, cut into 24 pieces. Serve warm or at room temperature.

24 (appetizer) servings.

Preparation time: 45 minutes. Ready to serve: 1 hour 20 minutes.

Per serving: 105 calories, 5 g total fat (1.5 g saturated fat), 5 mg cholesterol, 280 mg sodium, 1 g fiber.

SOUPS, SALADS & SIDES

Herbs can be used to infuse the broth or provide a flavorful finish to a soup; either way, they play a key role in making beautiful soup. Herbs are also integral in salads, and make a natural pairing with vegetables for superb side dishes. This chapter presents a selection of herbal possibilities on all these culinary fronts.

Herb Garden Salad, page 87

HARVEST "THYME" SQUASH SOUP

Pears contribute an underlying sweetness to this luxurious squash soup. A thyme-infused cream swirl gives it a beautiful finish. Try infusing milk or cream with thyme when you are making mashed potatoes or cream sauce.

1 tablespoon olive oil	1 cup water
2 cups sliced leeks, white and light green parts only	1/4 cup whipping cream
2 lb. butternut squash, seeded, cut into 2-inch cubes*	6 fresh thyme sprigs or 1 teaspoon dried
2 firm ripe pears, such as Bartlett or Anjou, cored, diced	1/4 cup low-fat plain yogurt or reduced-fat sour cream
2 garlic cloves, crushed	1 tablespoon fresh lemon juice
1 tablespoon chopped fresh thyme or 1 teaspoon dried	1/4 teaspoon salt
2 (14.5-oz.) cans reduced-sodium chicken broth	1/8 teaspoon freshly ground pepper
	Chopped fresh chives

❶ In 4- to 6-quart soup pot, heat oil over medium heat. Add leeks; cook 3 to 4 minutes or until tender, stirring frequently. Add squash, pears, garlic and chopped thyme; cook 1 minute, stirring constantly. Add broth and water; bring to a simmer. Reduce heat to low. Simmer, covered, 30 minutes or until squash is tender.

❷ Meanwhile, in small saucepan, heat cream until steaming. Remove from heat; add thyme sprigs. Cover and steep 20 minutes. Strain cream into small bowl, pressing on thyme to extract flavor. Add yogurt; whisk until smooth.

❸ Strain soup through colander into large bowl. Place solids in food processor; process until smooth. Return puree and broth to soup pot; heat through. Stir in lemon juice; season with salt and pepper. *(Soup can be prepared up to 2 days ahead. Cover and refrigerate.)*

❹ To serve, ladle soup into bowls; add large dollop (or several small dollops) of infused cream to each bowl. Draw tip of knife or toothpick through cream to make decorative swirls. Garnish with chives.

TIP *To make a squash easier to peel, try this trick: Pierce squash in several places with a fork or skewer and microwave on High for 2 minutes just to soften skin. Let stand for several minutes. Use a vegetable peeler or paring knife to remove skin.

8 (1-cup) servings.

Preparation time: 30 minutes. Ready to serve: 1 hour, 15 minutes.

Per serving: 145 calories, 5 g total fat (2 g saturated fat), 10 mg cholesterol, 525 mg sodium, 5 g fiber.

COUSCOUS SALAD WITH APRICOTS, PINE NUTS AND MINT

When you are cooking outdoors, coordinating side dishes can be tricky. You can avoid running between the outdoor grill and kitchen stove if you opt for a light but substantial grain salad instead of a traditional hot side dish. This couscous salad, which features a distinctive apricot dressing, is good with grilled chicken or lamb.

APRICOT DRESSING

- 1/4 cup apricot nectar
- 2 tablespoons extra-virgin olive oil
- 4 teaspoons white wine vinegar
- 1/2 teaspoon honey
- 2 (1/4-inch) slices fresh ginger, crushed
- 1 medium garlic clove, crushed
- 1/4 teaspoon salt
- 1/8 teaspoon freshly ground pepper

SALAD

- 1 cup couscous
- 1/4 cup chopped dried apricots
- 1/4 teaspoon salt
- 1 1/4 cups hot water
- 1/2 cup trimmed chopped scallions
- 1/3 cup slivered fresh mint
- 1/4 cup pine nuts, toasted (see TIP, page 54)

❶ In blender, combine apricot nectar, oil, vinegar, honey, ginger, garlic, 1/4 teaspoon salt and pepper; cover and process until blended. *(Dressing can be prepared up to 2 days ahead. Cover and refrigerate.)*

❷ In large bowl, combine couscous, dried apricots and 1/4 teaspoon salt. Pour in hot water. Let stand 20 minutes or until couscous is tender and water has been absorbed.

❸ Add scallions, mint and dressing to couscous mixture; toss gently to mix. Transfer to serving bowl and sprinkle with pine nuts. *(Salad can be held at room temperature for up to 45 minutes.)*

6 (3/4-cup) servings.

Preparation time: 30 minutes. Ready to serve: 40 minutes.

Per serving: 205 calories, 8 g total fat (1 g saturated fat), 0 mg cholesterol, 203 mg sodium, 3 g fiber.

PASTA, GRAINS & BEANS

Pasta with a heady basil pesto sauce is now a familiar and much-loved combination in America. But the possibilities for using herbs to enhance a variety of wholesome pasta, grain and bean dishes go much further. This chapter celebrates "pyramid" eating at its best.

Lenti-Orzo Stew, page 104

PEANUT NOODLES

A spicy peanut butter dressing creates a satisfying Asian noodle salad. The vibrant garnish of herbs and cucumber brings this salad to life.

DRESSING
- 1/2 cup natural peanut butter*
- 1/3 cup reduced-fat firm silken tofu
- 1/4 cup low-sodium soy sauce
- 3 tablespoons fresh lime juice
- 3 garlic cloves, minced
- 2 tablespoons packed brown sugar
- 3/4 teaspoon crushed red pepper

SALAD
- 1 (12-oz.) pkg. spaghetti
- 2 teaspoons toasted peanut oil or toasted sesame oil
- 1 cup grated carrots
- 1 small red bell pepper, finely diced
- 3/4 cup grated seedless (English) cucumber
- 1/4 cup slivered fresh cilantro
- 1/4 cup slivered fresh mint
- 4 scallions, chopped
- 3 tablespoons unsalted dry-roasted peanuts, chopped
- Lime wedges

❶ In food processor, combine peanut butter, tofu, soy sauce, lime juice, garlic, brown sugar and red pepper; process until smooth and creamy, stopping once or twice to scrape down sides of work bowl. Set aside. (*Dressing can be made ahead. Cover and refrigerate up to 2 days.*)

❷ Cook spaghetti according to package directions. Drain and rinse with cold running water. Drain again, shaking colander to release excess water. Transfer to large bowl. Drizzle with oil and toss to coat.

❸ Add carrot and bell pepper to spaghetti. Add dressing; toss to coat. Transfer to large shallow serving bowl. Sprinkle with cucumber, cilantro, mint, scallions and peanuts. Garnish with lime wedges.

TIP *Healthful silken tofu stretches the peanut butter and gives it a velvety consistency. Look for peanut butter labeled as natural; because it is not homogenized, it does not contain *trans* fatty acids.

6 (1-cup) servings.

Preparation time: 30 minutes. Ready to serve: 40 minutes.

Per serving: 445 calories, 16 g total fat (3 g saturated fat), 0 mg cholesterol, 750 mg sodium, 5.5 g fiber.

COUSCOUS WITH GRILLED VEGETABLES AND CHARMOULA SAUCE

Here is an elegant entrée for entertaining a group that includes both vegetarians and nonvegetarians — double the recipe, and supplement the vegetables with grilled chicken or tuna.

VEGETABLES

1 recipe *Moroccan Charmoula Sauce* (page 166)

1 (3/4-lb.) eggplant, cut into 3/8-inch slices

1 medium red bell pepper, seeded, cut into 8 wedges

1 medium zucchini, cut into 3/8-inch slices

1 large red onion, cut into 3/8-inch slices

6 plum tomatoes, halved lengthwise

Olive oil nonstick cooking spray

1/2 teaspoon salt

1/2 teaspoon freshly ground pepper

COUSCOUS

2 cups vegetable or reduced-sodium chicken broth

2 teaspoons extra-virgin olive oil

1/4 teaspoon salt

1/4 teaspoon freshly ground pepper

1 cup couscous

1/3 cup dried currants

1/3 cup slivered almonds, toasted (see TIP, page 164)

❶ Prepare Charmoula Sauce; set aside.

❷ Heat grill. Spray both sides of eggplant, bell pepper, zucchini, onion and tomatoes with olive oil nonstick cooking spray. Sprinkle with 1/2 teaspoon salt and 1/2 teaspoon pepper.

❸ Place vegetables on gas grill over medium-high heat or on charcoal grill 4 to 6 inches from medium-high coals. Cook 6 to 10 minutes, turning frequently and removing vegetables when they are browned and tender. (If desired, remove charred tomato skins.) Keep warm.

❹ In medium saucepan, combine 2 cups broth, 2 teaspoons oil, 1/4 teaspoon salt and 1/4 teaspoon pepper. Bring to a simmer. Remove from heat. Stir in couscous and currants; cover and let stand 5 minutes to plump. Fluff couscous with fork.

❺ Meanwhile, in small saucepan, heat sauce over medium heat until thoroughly heated, stirring occasionally.

❻ To serve, mound couscous in center of large platter. Surround with grilled vegetables. Drizzle sauce over vegetables and couscous. Sprinkle with almonds.

4 servings.

Preparation time: 30 minutes. Ready to serve: 50 minutes.

Per serving: 445 calories, 15 g total fat (2 g saturated fat), 0 mg cholesterol, 1,215 mg sodium, 9.5 g fiber.

SHRIMP RISOTTO WITH GREMOLADA

Here's one more example of how gremolada, the classic trio of parsley, lemon peel and garlic, gives a simple dish a special flourish.

1/3 cup chopped fresh Italian parsley
1 teaspoon freshly grated lemon peel
2 medium garlic cloves, minced
2 (14.5-oz.) cans reduced-sodium chicken broth
1/2 cup water
4 teaspoons olive oil
12 oz. shelled, deveined uncooked medium shrimp, each cut into 2 or 3 pieces
2 medium shallots, finely chopped
 Dash of crushed red pepper
1 cup Arborio rice
1/2 cup dry white wine
2 teaspoons fresh lemon juice
1/4 teaspoon freshly ground pepper

❶ In small bowl, combine parsley, lemon peel and garlic; toss with fork to mix.

❷ In large saucepan, combine chicken broth and water; bring to a simmer over medium heat. Reduce heat to low; keep broth at low simmer.

❸ In Dutch oven, heat 2 teaspoons oil over medium heat until hot. Add shrimp; cook about 2 minutes or until shrimp turn pink and opaque in center, stirring occasionally. Transfer to plate.

❹ Add remaining 2 teaspoons oil to Dutch oven. Add shallots and red pepper; cook 30 seconds to 1 minute or until shallots are tender, stirring constantly. Add rice; cook 30 seconds, stirring constantly. Add wine; cook about 30 seconds or until almost evaporated, stirring constantly. Add 1 cup of the hot broth; cook 1 to 2 minutes or until most of the liquid has been absorbed, stirring constantly. Continue to simmer 18 to 20 minutes, stirring frequently, adding broth about 1/2 cup at a time and waiting until most of it has been absorbed before adding more, until rice is just tender and risotto has a creamy consistency.

❺ Add shrimp; cook about 1 minute or until heated through. Remove risotto from heat. Stir in parsley mixture, lemon juice and pepper.

4 (1 1/4-cup) servings.
Preparation time: 15 minutes. Ready to serve: 40 minutes.
Per serving: 335 calories, 7 g total fat (1.5 g saturated fat), 120 mg cholesterol, 570 mg sodium, 1 g fiber.

SLOW-COOKER MEXICAN BEANS

Here is an easy way to cook basic beans to use for refried beans, soups or black beans and rice. The gentle, even heat of a slow cooker is ideal for beans and simulates an old-fashioned earthenware bean pot. There is a generous quantity of flavorful cooking broth to moisten refried beans or to cook rice.

2	cups black beans, rinsed
1	medium onion, chopped
2	garlic cloves, crushed, peeled
1	(4-inch-long) fresh epazote sprig or 1 teaspoon dried
5	cups boiling water
1½	teaspoons salt

❶ Place beans in large bowl; cover with cold water. Cover bowl; soak beans at room temperature at least 6 hours or overnight. (Or place beans in a large pot with enough water to cover by 2 inches. Bring to a boil over medium-high heat. Remove from heat and let stand 1 hour.)

❷ Drain beans and rinse thoroughly. Place in 3½-quart slow cooker. Add onion, garlic and epazote sprig. Add boiling water. Cook, covered, on High setting 3½ hours or until beans are almost tender.

❸ Add salt; cook an additional 15 to 30 minutes or until beans are tender. Remove and discard epazote sprig. (*Beans will keep, covered, in the refrigerator up to 3 days.*)

5 cups beans, 4 cups broth.

Preparation time: 10 minutes. Ready to serve: 4 hours, 10 minutes (not including soaking time).

Per ½-cup serving: 140 calories, 0.5 g total fat (0 g saturated fat), 0 mg cholesterol, 350 mg sodium, 7 g fiber.

CHEF'S NOTES:

• If you do not have a slow cooker, you can gently simmer the beans in a large heavy pot on the stovetop. Cook beans about 1½ hours, then add salt and simmer about 30 minutes longer.

• To make refried beans, soften some chopped onion and a few minced garlic cloves in a little canola oil in a large nonstick skillet. Add beans (with some of their broth) and cook, mashing with a wooden spoon until mixture has thickened. Serve, sprinkled with minced jalapeño chiles, slivered cilantro and crumbled farmer cheese. Accompany with toasted corn tortillas.

GREEN RICE

A rice pilaf seasoned with cilantro and mild chiles makes a perfect accompaniment to many Latin dishes.

2 teaspoons olive oil
1 medium onion, chopped
1 (4.5-oz.) can chopped green chiles
2 garlic cloves, minced
1 cup long-grain white rice
1 (14.5-oz.) can reduced-sodium chicken broth
3/4 cup chopped fresh cilantro
1/2 cup chopped trimmed scallions
1 tablespoon fresh lime juice
1/8 teaspoon salt
1/8 teaspoon freshly ground pepper

❶ In medium saucepan, heat oil over medium heat until hot. Add onion; cook about 2 to 3 minutes or until tender, stirring frequently. Add chiles and garlic; cook 1 minute, stirring frequently. Add rice; cook 1 minute, stirring constantly, until well mixed. Add broth; bring to a simmer over medium heat. Reduce heat to low; simmer, covered, about 20 minutes or until rice is tender and liquid has been absorbed. Remove from heat. Add cilantro, scallions, lime juice, salt and pepper; fluff and mix gently with rubber spatula.

4 (1-cup) servings.

Preparation time: 10 minutes. Ready to serve: 40 minutes.

Per serving: 245 calories, 3.5 g total fat (0.5 g saturated fat), 0 mg cholesterol, 570 mg sodium, 2 g fiber.

MEAT, POULTRY, FISH & SEAFOOD

Whether you are roasting, grilling, braising or poaching, herbs are integral to enhancing meat, poultry, fish and seafood. This chapter covers the basic techniques.

Pork Tenderloin with Apple, Thyme and Mustard Marinade, page 122

LEG OF LAMB WITH HERBES DE PROVENCE

Aromatic herbs, mustard and garlic make a delicious crust for a Sunday dinner lamb roast. Accompany with Herbed Goat Cheese Mashed Potatoes *(page 88) and steamed green beans.*

2 tablespoons grainy mustard	1 medium onion, sliced
2 tablespoons olive oil	1 medium carrot, sliced
2 tablespoons *Herbes de Provence* (page 14)	2/3 cup dry red wine
4 garlic cloves, minced	1 (14.5-oz.) can reduced-sodium chicken broth
1/2 teaspoon salt	1 tablespoon cornstarch
1/2 teaspoon freshly ground pepper	1 tablespoon water
1 (4 1/2- to 5 1/2-lb.) shank-half, bone-in leg of lamb	

❶ In small bowl, combine mustard, olive oil, *herbes de Provence*, garlic, salt and pepper; mix well. Rub mixture evenly over lamb. Place in shallow glass dish. Refrigerate, covered, at least 30 minutes or up to 4 hours.

❷ Heat oven to 425°F. Spray small roasting pan or large oven-safe skillet with nonstick cooking spray.

❸ Place onion and carrot slices in center of pan. Place lamb over vegetables. Bake 20 minutes. Reduce oven temperature to 350°F. Bake 45 minutes to 1 1/2 hours or until of desired doneness. Place lamb on cutting board; cover loosely with aluminum foil and let rest.

❹ Discard any charred vegetables. Place roasting pan with vegetables on stovetop over medium-high heat. Pour in wine; bring to a boil, stirring to scrape up any browned bits. Cook 2 to 3 minutes or until reduced by half. Add broth; bring to a boil. Cook 2 to 3 minutes to intensify flavor. Strain sauce into medium saucepan, Bring sauce to a simmer over medium-high heat. In small bowl, mix cornstarch and water; add to simmering sauce. Cook about 1 minute, whisking constantly, until slightly thickened. Keep warm. Carve lamb and serve with sauce.

6 servings.

Preparation time: 25 minutes. Ready to serve: 2 hours, 45 minutes.

Per serving: 445 calories, 22 g total fat (7 g saturated fat), 170 mg cholesterol, 535 mg sodium, 0.5 g fiber.

> **CHEF'S NOTE:**
> • Set the roast on a bed of sliced onions and carrots to make a vegetable "rack" that helps flavor the pan drippings for the pan sauce.

VIETNAMESE GRILLED CHICKEN THIGHS

Meaty chicken thighs are well suited to this intensely flavored Vietnamese marinade. You can certainly use bone-in chicken thighs (adjust cooking time accordingly — they will take 20 to 30 minutes) if you prefer, but boneless thighs are easy to eat and fun when they are secured on lemongrass "skewers" (page 19). Serve with steamed rice.

6 stalks fresh lemongrass	2 tablespoons fish sauce
2 serrano or jalapeño chiles, seeded, coarsely chopped	1 tablespoon canola oil
4 garlic cloves, crushed	8 boneless skinless chicken thighs (1¾ lb.), trimmed
2 tablespoons sugar	1 recipe *Papaya Relish* (page 157)
¼ cup fresh lime juice	Lime wedges

❶ Prepare 4 stalks lemongrass for lemongrass skewers (see page 19).

❷ Trim remaining 2 lemongrass stalks (see page 9); chop coarsely. In mini food processor, combine chopped lemongrass, chiles, garlic and sugar; pulse until finely chopped. Add lime juice, fish sauce and oil; process until mixture forms a chunky puree. Reserve ¼ cup of this mixture for basting.

❸ Place chicken in shallow glass dish. Add remaining lemongrass marinade; turn to coat. Refrigerate, covered, 30 minutes or up to 4 hours, turning occasionally.

❹ Meanwhile, prepare Papaya Relish.

❺ Heat grill. With metal skewer, poke 2 holes through each chicken thigh. Thread 2 chicken thighs onto each frozen lemongrass skewer. Strain reserved lemongrass mixture, pressing on solids to extract flavor; set aside for basting.

❻ Lightly oil grill rack. Place skewered chicken on gas grill over medium-high heat or on charcoal grill 4 to 6 inches from medium-hot coals. Cover grill and cook, turning once or twice and basting browned sides with reserved marinade, 12 to 15 minutes or until chicken is browned and no longer pink in center. Garnish with lime wedges. Serve with Papaya Relish.

4 servings.

Preparation time: 45 minutes. Ready to serve: 1 hour, 30 minutes.

Per serving: 280 calories, 10.5 g total fat (3 g saturated fat), 95 mg cholesterol, 345 mg sodium, 2 g fiber.

> **CHEF'S NOTE:**
> • This marinade is also delicious with quail. Split quail before marinating and grilling.

PORK TENDERLOIN WITH APPLE, THYME AND MUSTARD MARINADE

A little sweetness in a marinade enhances flavors and promotes browning. In this marinade, apple juice concentrate provides the sweet element and offers a good fruity complement to the thyme. The marinade is also good with chicken.

PORK AND MARINADE

- 1/4 cup frozen apple juice concentrate, thawed
- 2 tablespoons Dijon mustard
- 2 tablespoons chopped fresh thyme or 2 teaspoons dried
- 1 tablespoon olive oil
- 4 garlic cloves, minced
- 1 teaspoon black peppercorns, crushed
- 1 1/2 lb. pork tenderloin

PORT VINAIGRETTE

- 3 tablespoons port wine
- 2 tablespoons balsamic vinegar
- 1 tablespoon extra-virgin olive oil
- 1 1/2 teaspoons Dijon mustard
- 2 tablespoons finely chopped shallot
- 1/4 teaspoon salt
- 1/8 teaspoon freshly ground pepper

❶ In small bowl, whisk apple juice concentrate, 2 tablespoons mustard, thyme, 1 tablespoon oil, garlic and peppercorns. Reserve 1/4 cup of mixture for basting. Place tenderloins in shallow glass dish. Pour remaining marinade over pork; turn to coat. Refrigerate, covered, at least 30 minutes or up to 8 hours, turning several times.

❷ Heat grill. In small bowl, make port vinaigrette: combine port, vinegar, 1 tablespoon oil, 1 1/2 teaspoons mustard, shallot, salt and pepper; whisk to blend.

❸ Lightly oil grill rack. Place tenderloins on gas grill over medium-high heat or on charcoal grill 4 to 6 inches from medium-hot coals. Cover grill and cook 20 to 25 minutes, turning occasionally and basting with reserved marinade until tenderloins are browned and internal temperature reaches 150°F. Transfer tenderloins to clean cutting board. Cover tenderloins loosely with aluminum foil; let rest 5 to 10 minutes.

❹ Carve tenderloins into 1/2-inch slices. Serve with port vinaigrette.

6 servings.

Preparation time: 20 minutes. Ready to serve: 1 hour, 20 minutes.

Per serving: 215 calories, 9 g total fat (2 g saturated fat), 70 mg cholesterol, 200 mg sodium, 0.5 g fiber.

CHEF'S NOTE:
- Substitute chopped fresh rosemary for fresh thyme.

GRILLED SALMON WITH MINT AND GINGER CHUTNEY

Accompany the salmon with a basmati rice pilaf and green peas simmered with scallions.

1 recipe *Mint and Ginger Chutney* (page 161)
4 (5-oz.) salmon fillets (1 inch thick)
2 teaspoons canola oil
3/4 teaspoon salt
1/2 teaspoon freshly ground pepper
4 fresh mint leaves
  Fresh mint sprigs
  Lime wedges

❶ Prepare Mint and Ginger Chutney; set aside.

❷ Heat grill. Brush salmon with oil; sprinkle with salt and pepper. Press 1 mint leaf onto curved skinless side of each piece of salmon.

❸ Place salmon, skin side up, on gas grill over medium-high heat or on charcoal grill 4 to 6 inches from medium-hot coals. Cover grill and cook, turning once, 8 to 10 minutes or until fish just begins to flake. Garnish with fresh mint and lime wedges. Serve with Mint and Ginger Chutney.

4 servings.

Preparation time: 20 minutes. Ready to serve: 30 minutes.

Per serving: 240 calories, 9.5 g total fat (2 g saturated fat), 80 mg cholesterol, 670 mg sodium, 1 g fiber.

CHEF'S NOTE:
• Mint leaves pressed on the salmon help protect the delicate fillet from the heat of the grill. The mint adds a subtle fragrance as well.

SPRING ROLLS WITH SHRIMP AND RICE NOODLE FILLING

These lively and light Vietnamese spring rolls make ideal hot-weather fare. Cilantro and mint provide a fresh contrast to the spicy dipping sauce.

DRESSING

- ½ cup pineapple juice
- 2 tablespoons low-sodium soy sauce
- 1 tablespoon fish sauce
- 2 tablespoons rice vinegar
- 1 tablespoon canola oil
- 1 teaspoon Thai green curry paste
- 1 teaspoon packed brown sugar
- 3 tablespoons coarsely chopped fresh ginger
- 2 medium garlic cloves, crushed

SPRING ROLLS

- 2 oz. thin rice noodles or rice sticks
- 12 rice-paper wrappers
- 12 large leaves Boston lettuce
- 1 lb. shelled, deveined cooked medium shrimp, tails removed
- ¾ cup grated carrots (2 to 3 medium)
- ¾ cup finely diced fresh pineapple
- ¾ cup slivered fresh cilantro
- ¾ cup slivered fresh mint

❶ In blender, combine pineapple juice, soy sauce, fish sauce, rice vinegar, oil, curry paste, brown sugar, ginger and garlic; process until well blended. (*Dressing can be made ahead. Cover and refrigerate up to 2 days.*)

❷ In large bowl, cover rice noodles with boiling water; stir to immerse and separate strands. Let soak 5 minutes. Drain noodles; rinse with cold water. Drain again, shaking colander to release excess water. Return noodles to bowl. Add 2 tablespoons of the dressing; toss to coat.

❸ Shortly before serving, assemble spring rolls. Set all prepared filling ingredients out on counter. Set out large bowl of warm water, baking sheet, serving platter and damp kitchen towel. Working with 2 rice paper wrappers at a time, dip into warm water 10 to 20 seconds or until softened. Shake off moisture and lay out on baking sheet. Place one lettuce leaf on bottom third of each wrapper. Top each lettuce leaf with about 2 tablespoons rice noodle mixture, 3 or 4 shrimp, generous 1 tablespoon carrot, generous 1 tablespoon pineapple, 1 tablespoon cilantro and 1 tablespoon mint. Fold bottom of wrapper over to partially cover filling. Fold sides over filling and continue to roll wrapper into a cylinder to seal.

❹ Place on platter. Cover with damp kitchen towel to prevent spring rolls from drying out. Repeat with remaining rice paper wrappers and filling ingredients. Serve with remaining dressing as dipping sauce.

6 servings.

Preparation time: 1 hour, 30 minutes. Ready to serve: 1 hour, 30 minutes.

CHEF'S NOTES:

- Fish sauce, green curry paste, rice vermicelli and rice paper wrappers can be found in the Asian section of many supermarkets, health food stores, Asian markets.

- For an interesting presentation, wrap each spring roll with a chive ribbon (see page 16).

- Whole shrimp look attractive. But for easier wrapping, chop them coarsely and use about 2 tablespoons per roll.

Per serving: 210 calories, 3.5 g total fat (0.5 g saturated fat), 155 mg cholesterol, 490 mg sodium, 2 g fiber.

NORTH AFRICAN TUNA KABOBS

Lemon wedges give these kabobs an interesting presentation, but when the kabobs are cooked, the grilled lemon wedges can also be used for squeezing extra lemon juice over the tuna. Serve these kabobs over couscous and accompany with a selection of grilled vegetables.

½ cup chopped fresh cilantro	1½ teaspoons paprika
½ cup chopped fresh Italian parsley	¾ teaspoon salt
4 garlic cloves, minced	½ teaspoon freshly ground pepper
½ cup extra-virgin olive oil	1¾ lb. tuna steak (1¼-inch thick),
⅓ cup fresh lemon juice	cut into 1¼-inch chunks
2 teaspoons ground cumin	2 lemons, each cut into 6 wedges

❶ In small bowl, whisk together cilantro, parsley, garlic, olive oil, lemon juice, cumin, paprika, salt and pepper. Reserve ½ cup of this mixture to serve as sauce. Place tuna in a shallow glass dish. Pour remaining marinade over tuna; turn to coat. Refrigerate, covered, at least 20 minutes or up to 1 hour, turning occasionally. Cover and keep reserved sauce at room temperature.

❷ Heat grill. Thread 1 piece of tuna, 1 lemon wedge, 2 pieces of tuna, another lemon wedge and final piece of tuna onto 10- or 12-inch skewer. Repeat with remaining tuna and lemon wedges to make a total of 6 kabobs.

❸ Lightly oil grill rack. Place kabobs on gas grill over high heat or on charcoal grill 4 to 6 inches from hot coals. Cover grill and cook, turning occasionally, 7 to 9 minutes or until tuna is browned and just begins to flake. Serve with reserved sauce.

6 servings.

Preparation time: 30 minutes. Ready to serve: 1 hour.

Per serving: 300 calories, 20.5 g total fat (4 g saturated fat), 80 mg cholesterol, 295 mg sodium, 1 g fiber.

AEGEAN HALIBUT STEW

This fish stew is fragrant with the flavors of the Greek islands. It is a one-pot meal with a generous amount of lemon-dill avgolemono sauce. Serve with crusty bread to mop up the sauce.

2	teaspoons olive oil	1	lb. halibut fillet, skin removed, cut into 1¼-inch chunks
1	medium onion, chopped		
2	garlic cloves, minced	1	large egg
2½	cups reduced-sodium chicken broth	3	tablespoons fresh lemon juice
		¼	cup chopped fresh dill
1	lb. Yukon Gold potatoes, cut into 2½ x ¾-inch wedges	¼	teaspoon salt
		⅛	teaspoon freshly ground pepper
6	medium carrots, cut into 2 x ½-inch sticks		Lemon wedges
			Fresh dill sprigs

❶ In Dutch oven, heat oil over medium heat until hot. Add onion; cook about 2 minutes or until tender, stirring constantly. Add garlic; cook 30 seconds. Add broth; bring to a simmer. Add potatoes and carrots; return to a simmer. Cook, covered, about 15 minutes or until vegetables are tender. With slotted spoon, transfer vegetables to serving bowl. Cover and keep warm.

❷ Add halibut to Dutch oven. Reduce heat to medium-low; cook, covered, 5 to 7 minutes or until halibut is opaque and begins to flake. With slotted spoon, transfer fish to bowl with vegetables. Cover and keep warm.

❸ In medium bowl, whisk egg and lemon juice. Stir in chopped dill. Gradually whisk a little of the hot cooking liquid into egg mixture; pour egg mixture into remaining cooking liquid in Dutch oven. Cook, stirring constantly, over medium heat 2 to 3 minutes or until slightly thickened and temperature reaches 160°F. Season with salt and pepper. Spoon sauce over halibut and vegetables. Garnish with lemon wedges and fresh dill.

4 (1½-cup) servings.

Preparation time: 30 minutes. Ready to serve: 50 minutes.

Per serving: 320 calories, 6 g total fat (1.5 g saturated fat), 115 mg cholesterol, 605 mg sodium, 6 g fiber.

CHEF'S NOTES:
- You can also use halibut steaks. Just cut around the bones to separate fillet portions. Purchase about 1⅔ pounds halibut steaks to allow for loss during filleting and trimming.
- You can substitute other firm fish, such as monkfish or sea bass.

DESSERTS & BEVERAGES

The only herb routinely paired with sweet flavors is mint. But some nontraditional dessert herbs, such as basil and rosemary, also complement fruit flavors in delightful ways. This chapter offers a selection of refreshing herbal beverages and fragrant sweet endings.

Peach-Blackberry Compote with Basil Syrup, page 145

139

ROSEMARY-SCENTED LEMON LOAF

Rosemary works well in sweet preparations and is a natural partner with lemon. Enjoy this fragrant loaf with afternoon tea.

2¼	cups all-purpose flour
1½	teaspoons baking powder
½	teaspoon baking soda
½	teaspoon salt
2	large eggs
1	cup sugar
⅓	cup butter, melted, or light olive oil
4	teaspoons chopped fresh rosemary
2	teaspoons freshly grated lemon peel
1	teaspoon vanilla
¾	cup buttermilk

❶ Heat oven to 350°F. Spray 9x5-inch loaf pan with cooking spray.

❷ In medium bowl, whisk flour, baking powder, baking soda and salt.

❸ In large bowl, combine eggs and sugar; beat at high speed 3 to 5 minutes or until pale in color and thickened. Add butter, rosemary, lemon peel and vanilla; beat at low speed just until blended. With rubber spatula, alternately fold in flour mixture and buttermilk, beginning and ending with flour. Spread batter evenly in pan.

❹ Bake 40 to 45 minutes or until golden and toothpick inserted near center comes out clean. Cool in pan on wire rack 5 minutes. Loosen edges; turn loaf out onto rack. Cool completely.

12 servings.

Preparation time: 25 minutes. Ready to serve: 1 hour, 45 minutes.

Per serving: 215 calories, 6.5 g total fat (3.5 g saturated fat), 50 mg cholesterol, 270 mg sodium, 0.5 g fiber.

BLOODY MARY MIX

This savory smoothie makes a healthful "pick-me-up" snack or delicious base for a vodka-laced Bloody Mary cocktail. In addition to the traditional Bloody Mary seasonings, it is doctored with fresh tomato and herbs.

1½	cups chilled tomato-vegetable juice blend
1	medium tomato, seeded, coarsely chopped
2	tablespoons coarsely chopped fresh lovage*
1	tablespoon fresh lime juice
1	teaspoon Worcestershire sauce
¼ to ½	teaspoon hot pepper sauce
2	ice cubes
	Fresh lovage sprigs

❶ In blender, combine tomato-vegetable juice, tomato, lovage, lime juice, Worcestershire sauce, hot pepper sauce and ice cubes. Cover and blend until smooth. Pour into glasses. Garnish each serving with fresh lovage.

3 (6-oz.) servings.

Preparation time: 15 minutes. Ready to serve: 15 minutes.

Per serving: 35 calories, 0.5 g total fat (0 g saturated fat), 0 mg cholesterol, 470 mg sodium, 1.5 g fiber.

CHEF'S NOTE:

- Lovage contributes a very distinctive and complementary celery-like flavor to this Bloody Mary Mix. Unfortunately, unless you are an avid gardener, lovage can be difficult to find. You can substitute Italian parsley or basil for lovage.

HERB CIDER

Infusing apple cider with thyme creates a hot beverage that combines the soothing qualities of herb tea and the warming properties of spiced apple cider.

  8 fresh thyme sprigs
1/2 teaspoon black peppercorns
  4 cups pasteurized apple cider

❶ Place thyme and peppercorns in tea infuser or tie in cheesecloth bag. In large saucepan, bring cider just to a simmer over medium-high heat. Remove from heat. Place tea infuser in cider; cover and steep 30 minutes. Remove infuser; reheat cider until steaming. Serve hot.

4 (1-cup) servings.

Preparation time: 5 minutes. Ready to serve: 35 minutes.

Per serving: 115 calories, 0.5 g total fat (0 g saturated fat), 0 mg cholesterol, 5 mg sodium, 0.5 g fiber.

PEACH-BLACKBERRY COMPOTE WITH BASIL SYRUP

There is a secret ingredient in this sophisticated summer fruit compote — it is fresh basil, which has a special affinity with peaches. The basil garnish is a clue to the subtle — yet distinctive — flavor in the syrup.

1/4	cup sugar
3	tablespoons dry white wine
3	fresh basil sprigs
2	(2-inch) strips orange peel (thin colored portion only)
3	cups sliced peeled peaches (1½ lb.)*
1	cup fresh blackberries, rinsed
1	tablespoon fresh lemon juice
	Fresh basil sprigs

❶ In small saucepan, simmer sugar and wine over medium heat. Remove from heat; stir in 3 basil sprigs and orange peel. Cover and steep 30 minutes.

❷ Strain syrup into small bowl, pressing on basil and orange peel to release flavor.

❸ In large bowl, combine peaches, blackberries and lemon juice. Add basil-infused syrup; toss gently to coat. Garnish with basil sprigs.

TIP *To peel peaches, dip them into boiling water for a few seconds, and then slip off skin.

4 (1-cup) servings.

Preparation time: 20 minutes. Ready to serve: 50 minutes.

Per serving: 125 calories, 0.5 g total fat (0 g saturated fat), 0 mg cholesterol, 0 mg sodium, 4.5 g fiber.

HONEY-LAVENDER PLUM GRATIN

Infuse lavender blossoms into the milk for a delicate perfume. This honey-sweetened, lavender-scented custard marries well with summer plums. A quick pass under the broiler to caramelize the top creates a simple, elegant dessert. Note that because the custard is stabilized with cornstarch, you can let it reach a gentle simmer.

CUSTARD*
- 3/4 cup reduced-fat milk
- 3/4 teaspoon unsprayed fresh lavender blossoms or 1/4 teaspoon dried
- 2 egg yolks
- 2 tablespoons honey
- 1 teaspoon cornstarch
- 1/2 teaspoon vanilla**

FRUIT AND TOPPING
- 4 medium plums, quartered, pitted
- 2 tablespoons sugar

❶ In small saucepan, heat milk over medium heat until steaming. Remove from heat. Add lavender; cover and steep 30 minutes.

❷ Pass milk through fine sieve into medium bowl. Return strained milk to saucepan; reheat until steaming.

❸ In medium bowl, whisk egg yolks, honey and cornstarch until smooth. Gradually add hot milk, whisking until blended. Return mixture to saucepan over medium heat. Cook 1 1/2 to 2 minutes or until slightly thickened and starting to bubble gently, whisking constantly. Transfer to clean medium bowl; whisk in vanilla. Cover loosely; refrigerate at least 1 hour or until chilled. (*Custard can be made ahead. Cover and refrigerate up to 2 days.*)

❹ Heat broiler. Spray 11x7-inch oval gratin dish or 4 individual gratin dishes with cooking spray. Spoon custard evenly over bottom of gratin dishes. Arrange plums, skin side down, in single layer over custard. Sprinkle sugar evenly over plums. Broil 5 to 7 minutes or until plums are lightly caramelized. Serve immediately.

TIP *You can also use the custard as a sauce for fresh raspberries or figs.

TIP **If vanilla bean is available, this is a great opportunity to use it. Replace the vanilla extract with a 3-inch piece of vanilla bean. Make a lengthwise slit in the bean with tip of sharp knife, scrape out the seeds and drop the whole bean into milk along with the lavender in step 1; let steep.

4 servings.

Preparation time: 25 minutes. Ready to serve: 2 hours, 15 minutes.

Per serving: 150 calories, 4 g total fat (1.5 g saturated fat), 110 mg cholesterol, 25 mg sodium, 1 g fiber.

RHUBARB FOOL WITH ANGELICA

Vanilla yogurt and a touch of whipped cream enrich a tart rhubarb compote in this old-fashioned fool. Angelica, which is traditionally used to mellow and enhance rhubarb, contributes a pleasant herbal note.

1	lb. fresh rhubarb, stem ends trimmed, cut into 1/2-inch lengths (3 1/2 cups)
1/3	cup sugar
2	tablespoons fresh orange juice
2	tablespoons finely diced angelica stems*
1 1/4	cups low-fat vanilla yogurt
1/3	cup whipping cream
6	strawberries, hulled, sliced
	Fresh mint sprigs

❶ In medium saucepan, combine rhubarb, sugar, orange juice and angelica. Cook over medium heat 7 to 9 minutes, stirring frequently, until rhubarb is tender and mixture has broken down into chunky puree. Transfer puree to medium bowl; cover loosely and refrigerate about 2 hours or until completely cooled.

❷ Line sieve or colander with cheesecloth; set over medium bowl at least 1/2 inch from bowl. Spoon yogurt into sieve. Cover; drain in refrigerator 1 1/2 to 2 hours.

❸ Meanwhile, place small bowl and beaters in freezer to chill.

❹ Discard whey that has drained from yogurt. Add drained yogurt to rhubarb; mix gently with rubber spatula. In chilled bowl, whip cream to soft peaks. Add to rhubarb-yogurt mixture; fold gently to mix, leaving distinct swirls. Spoon into 6 dessert glasses or bowls. (*Dessert can be made ahead. Cover and refrigerate up to 1 day.*) Garnish each serving with strawberry slices and mint sprigs.

6 (1/2-cup) servings.

Preparation time: 20 minutes. Ready to serve: 2 hours, 30 minutes.

Per serving: 145 calories, 4.5 g total fat (3 g saturated fat), 15 mg cholesterol, 35 mg sodium, 1 g fiber.

CHEF'S NOTE:
- Angelica is a delightful addition to any rhubarb dish, but it is not terribly common or easy to find. If it is not available, just leave it out; add an extra tablespoon of sugar instead.

TUNISIAN MINT TEA

While traveling in Tunisia, I discovered this delightful way to serve tea. Green tea is infused with mint leaves and served in a pretty glass. The special Tunisian touch is a garnish of pine nuts. The result is pure refreshment.

2   green tea bags
⅓   cup fresh mint sprigs
5   cups boiling water
1   tablespoon pine nuts, toasted (see TIP, page 54)
    Fresh mint sprigs
    Sugar, if desired

❶ Warm teapot by rinsing with boiling water. Place tea bags and ⅓ cup mint sprigs in teapot; pour in 5 cups boiling water. Cover and steep 5 minutes. Pour tea into individual glasses. Float a few pine nuts in each glass. Garnish each serving with mint sprigs. Sweeten with sugar.

6 (¾-cup) servings.

Preparation time: 10 minutes. Ready to serve: 15 minutes.

Per serving: 9 calories, 1 g total fat (0 g saturated fat), 0 mg cholesterol, 5 mg sodium, 0 g fiber.

STRAWBERRY SHORTCAKES WITH LEMON VERBENA CREAM

Here is a lightened-up version of a classic. Instead of straight whipped cream, the topping is made from vanilla yogurt and just enough real whipped cream to lighten the texture and contribute a luxurious taste. A whisper of lemon verbena adds a sophisticated and elegant note.

LEMON-VERBENA CREAM
1½ cups low-fat vanilla yogurt
½ cup whipping cream
4 teaspoons very finely chopped fresh lemon verbena

SHORTCAKES
2 cups all-purpose flour
2 tablespoons plus 2 teaspoons sugar
1 tablespoon baking powder
½ teaspoon baking soda
½ teaspoon salt
6 tablespoons butter, cut into small pieces
1 cup buttermilk
2 teaspoons reduced-fat milk

STRAWBERRY FILLING
6 cups (1½ lb.) strawberries, hulled, sliced
2 tablespoons sugar
Fresh lemon verbena sprigs

❶ Line sieve or colander with cheesecloth; set over medium bowl at least ½ inch from bottom. Spoon yogurt into sieve. Cover; drain in refrigerator 1½ hours. Meanwhile, place small bowl and beaters in freezer to chill. In chilled bowl with chilled beaters, whip cream to soft peaks. Push to one side of bowl. Discard whey that has drained from yogurt. Add drained yogurt and lemon verbena to whipped cream. With rubber spatula, fold gently to mix. (*Cream can be made ahead. Cover and refrigerate up to 8 hours.*)

❷ Heat oven to 425°F. Spray baking sheet with cooking spray.

❸ In large bowl, combine flour, 2 tablespoons sugar, baking powder, baking soda and salt; whisk to blend. Using pastry blender or fingertips, cut in butter until mixture crumbles. Make a well in center of flour mixture; add buttermilk, stirring with fork, just until dough clumps together. Turn out onto lightly floured surface; knead several times. Roll or pat dough ¾ inch thick. Using a 3- or 3½-inch round cutter, cut out circles. Arrange shortcakes 1 inch apart on baking sheet. Gather scraps; reroll. Brush tops with milk; sprinkle with remaining 2 teaspoons sugar.

❹ Bake shortcakes 15 to 20 minutes or until golden brown. Transfer to wire rack; cool at least 10 minutes. Meanwhile, in medium bowl, combine strawberries and 2 tablespoons sugar; toss gently to coat. Let stand about 20 minutes or until strawberries give off juice.

❺ Just before serving, assemble shortcakes: Using serrated knife, split 6 shortcakes horizontally. Place shortcake bottoms on individual plates. Spoon about ⅓ cup strawberries and juice over each shortcake bottom. Top each with scant ¼ cup lemon verbena cream. Replace shortcake tops. Place dollop of the remaining cream on each shortcake. Spoon remaining strawberries and juice over top. Garnish with lemon verbena sprigs.

6 servings.

Preparation time: 50 minutes. Ready to serve: 2 hours, 30 minutes.

Per serving: 455 calories, 20 g total fat (12 g saturated fat), 60 mg cholesterol, 700 mg sodium, 3 g fiber.

SPARKLING MINT LIMEADE

For pure refreshment, nothing beats homemade limeade or lemonade. In this version, the citrus base is infused with herbs and diluted with sparkling water for a lively finish.

1	cup fresh mint sprigs, plus more for garnish
1¼	cups fresh lime juice
⅔	cup sugar
	Ice cubes
3	cups (750 ml) chilled sparkling seltzer or soda water

❶ In medium bowl, bruise mint with pestle or wooden spoon to release fragrance. Add lime juice and sugar; stir to dissolve sugar. Cover and refrigerate at least 2 hours or up to 8 hours.

❷ Strain lime juice mixture, pressing on mint sprigs to extract flavor. To serve, place several ice cubes in each of 4 tall glasses. Pour ⅓ cup lime juice mixture into each glass; top off with ¾ cup sparkling water. Garnish each serving with a mint sprig.

4 (1-cup) servings.

Preparation time: 20 minutes. Ready to serve: 2 hours, 20 minutes.

Per serving: 145 calories, 0 g total fat (0 g saturated fat), 0 mg cholesterol, 55 mg sodium, 0.5 g fiber.

CHEF'S NOTES:

- To make lemonade, substitute rosemary sprigs for mint, lemon juice for lime juice, and reduce sugar to ½ cup. Garnish with rosemary sprigs.
- Whether you're serving lemonade or limeade, dip the edge of each glass in honey, then sugar.

Sauces & Condiments

Herbs build terrific flavor, so it is not surprising that they play a key role in a wide variety of sauces and condiments. This chapter serves as a handy reference, providing a selection of pestos, compound butters, mayonnaise-based sauces and relishes to brighten your meals.

No-Cook Summer Tomato Sauce, page 168

HEALTH-CONSCIOUS BASIL PESTO

Silken tofu is an effective replacement for much of the olive oil in a traditional pesto. Sneaking some tofu into a pesto is an easy way to include more beneficial soy protein in your diet.

1	large garlic clove, crushed
1/2	teaspoon salt
1 1/2	cups lightly packed fresh basil leaves
1/4	cup pine nuts, toasted (see TIP, page 54)
1/8	teaspoon freshly ground pepper
	Dash of crushed red pepper
1/2	cup reduced-fat firm silken tofu
1	tablespoon extra-virgin olive oil
1/4	cup (1 oz.) freshly grated Parmesan cheese

❶ Using mortar and pestle or side of chef's knife, mash garlic and salt into a paste. Transfer to food processor. Add basil, pine nuts, ground pepper and red pepper; process until finely chopped. Add tofu and oil; process until smooth and creamy. Add Parmesan cheese; pulse several times to blend. (*Pesto can be made ahead. Place sheet of plastic wrap directly on surface to prevent discoloration; refrigerate up to 2 days or freeze up to 6 months.*)

3/4 cup.

Preparation time: 10 minutes. Ready to serve: 10 minutes.

Per tablespoon: 45 calories, 4 g total fat (1 g saturated fat), 2 mg cholesterol, 290 mg sodium, 0.5 g fiber.

TRADITIONAL BASIL PESTO

Pesto has become a standby in American kitchens. A stash of pesto in the freezer is one of the best ways to preserve the taste of summer. Use it as a stuffing for boneless chicken breasts, toss it with pasta or top a pizza with it.

4 cups lightly packed fresh basil leaves
1/2 cup pine nuts, toasted (see TIP, page 54)
3 garlic cloves, crushed
1/2 teaspoon salt
1/4 teaspoon freshly ground pepper
1/4 cup extra-virgin olive oil
3/4 cup (3 oz.) freshly grated Parmesan cheese

> **CHEF'S NOTE:**
> • If using pesto for grilled pizza, bring to room temperature before spreading over crust.

❶ In food processor, combine basil, pine nuts, garlic, salt and pepper; process until pine nuts are ground. With motor running, gradually add oil through feed tube, processing until mixture forms a paste. Add Parmesan cheese; pulse until blended. (*Pesto can be made ahead. Place sheet of plastic wrap directly on surface to prevent discoloration; refrigerate up to 2 days or freeze up to 6 months.*)

1 1/3 cups.

Preparation time: 10 minutes. Ready to serve: 10 minutes.

Per tablespoon: 60 calories, 5.5 g total fat (1.5 g saturated fat), 5 mg cholesterol, 135 mg sodium, 0.5 g fiber.

PAPAYA RELISH

Here's a refreshing accompaniment to Asian grilled fare. Substitute mango for papaya, if you like.

2 garlic cloves, crushed
2 teaspoons sugar
1/4 teaspoon salt
2 tablespoons rice vinegar

1/2 teaspoon hot pepper sauce
1 firm papaya, seeded, diced
1/2 cup diced red onion
1/2 cup slivered fresh cilantro

❶ Using mortar and pestle or with side of chef's knife, mash garlic, sugar and salt into a paste; transfer to medium bowl. Whisk in vinegar and hot pepper sauce. Add papaya, onion and cilantro; toss gently to mix. Serve within 1 hour.

1 1/2 cups.

Preparation time: 20 minutes. Ready to serve: 20 minutes.

Per (1/4-cup) serving. 35 calories, 0 g total fat (0 g saturated fat), 0 mg cholesterol, 100 mg sodium, 1 g fiber.

QUICK TOMATO SAUCE

This basic tomato sauce is so easy, it is hard to imagine why anyone would bother with prepared sauces that are frequently too sweet and "cooked" tasting. Peppery marjoram gives a basic tomato sauce character and a meaty taste. Use this sauce for pizzas and pasta, or serve with fish. Note that if you are making the sauce to use in a dish that highlights other herbs, omit the marjoram.

1	tablespoon olive oil
4	garlic cloves, minced
1/8	teaspoon crushed red pepper
2	(14.5-oz.) cans diced tomatoes, undrained
1 to 2	tablespoons chopped fresh marjoram or 1 to 2 teaspoons dried, if desired
	Dash of salt
1/8	teaspoon freshly ground pepper

❶ In large saucepan, heat oil over medium-low heat until warm. Add garlic and red pepper; cook 30 seconds to 1 minute or until tender and fragrant but not colored, stirring constantly. Add tomatoes and 1 tablespoon marjoram; mash with potato masher. Bring to a simmer. Cook, uncovered, 20 to 25 minutes or until thickened, stirring and mashing occasionally. Season with salt and pepper. Taste and add more marjoram, if desired (*Sauce can be made ahead. Cover and refrigerate up to 4 days or freeze up to 3 months.*)

2¼ cups.

Preparation time: 10 minutes. Ready to serve: 35 minutes.

Per ¼ cup serving: 35 calories, 1.5 g total fat (0 g saturated fat), 0 mg cholesterol, 175 mg sodium, 1 g fiber.

CHEF'S NOTE:

• If marjoram is not available, substitute oregano. You can also flavor the sauce with ⅓ cup slivered fresh basil, added at the end of cooking.

MINT AND GINGER CHUTNEY

If mint is taking over your garden, take advantage and make up a batch of this bright, lively herb chutney. Serve with salmon, lamb chops or as an accompaniment to curries.

3   cups lightly packed fresh mint leaves
1   medium jalapeño chile, seeded, coarsely chopped
4   teaspoons coarsely chopped fresh ginger
1   tablespoon sugar
1/2   teaspoon salt
2   garlic cloves, crushed
1/3   cup plain nonfat yogurt
3   tablespoons rice vinegar

❶ In food processor, combine mint, chile, ginger, sugar, salt and 1/2 teaspoon salt; process until finely chopped. Add yogurt and vinegar; process until mixture forms a creamy sauce, stopping to scrape down sides of bowl several times. (*Sauce can be made ahead. Place sheet of plastic wrap directly on surface to prevent discoloration; refrigerate up to 2 days.*) Serve at room temperature.

3/4 cup.

Preparation time: 10 minutes. Ready to serve: 10 minutes.

Per tablespoon: 15 calories, 0 g total fat (0 g saturated fat), 0 mg cholesterol, 105 mg sodium, 0 g fiber.

PARSLEY-WALNUT PESTO

Requiring just a few basic ingredients you may have on hand, this easy sauce for pasta makes a handy standby for busy nights when the refrigerator seems bare. The proportion of nuts to herbs is higher than a traditional basil pesto. When this pesto is thinned with some pasta cooking water, it becomes a delicious garlicky walnut cream. This recipe makes about the right amount for 12 ounces of pasta.

- 1 cup lightly packed fresh Italian parsley leaves
- 3/4 cup walnuts, toasted*
- 2 garlic cloves, crushed
- 1/4 teaspoon salt
- 1/4 teaspoon freshly ground pepper
- 1/4 cup extra-virgin olive oil
- 1/2 cup (2 oz.) freshly grated Parmesan cheese

❶ In food processor, combine parsley, walnuts, garlic, salt and pepper; process until walnuts are ground. With motor running, gradually add oil, processing until mixture forms a paste. Add Parmesan cheese; pulse several times until blended. (*Pesto can be made ahead. Place sheet of plastic wrap directly on surface to prevent discoloration; refrigerate up to 2 days or freeze up to 6 months.*)

TIP *To toast walnuts, spread on baking sheet; bake at 375°F for 7 to 10 minutes or until fragrant. Transfer to small bowl to cool. Or in small dry skillet, toast walnuts over medium-low heat 3 to 4 minutes or until fragrant, stirring constantly. Transfer to small bowl to cool.

3/4 cup.

Preparation time: 20 minutes. Ready to serve: 20 minutes.

Per tablespoon: 105 calories, 10 g total fat (2 g saturated fat), 5 mg cholesterol, 190 mg sodium, 0.5 g fiber.

SHALLOT-MUSTARD HERB BUTTER

Compound butters are one of the simplest and most satisfying ways to embellish grilled foods. Traditional recipes use all butter, but I have found that I can lighten the butter by whipping in an equal proportion of flavorful olive oil, thereby improving the ratio of healthful mono-unsaturated fats to saturated fats. Serve with grilled fish steaks, veal or lamb chops, or beef steaks.

¼ cup butter, softened
¼ cup extra-virgin olive oil
2 tablespoons Dijon mustard
4 teaspoons fresh lemon juice
2 tablespoons finely chopped shallot
2 tablespoons chopped fresh Italian parsley
¼ teaspoon freshly ground pepper

> **CHEF'S NOTES:**
> • One of the easiest ways to preserve fresh herbs is to make up a batch of compound butter and freeze it in small portions. Place a portion of compound butter in a sheet of plastic wrap, roll into a cylinder and secure the plastic wrap.
> • For basil butter: Substitute basil for parsley and orange juice for lemon juice.
> • For tarragon butter: Substitute tarragon for parsley.
> • For *fines herbes* butter: Substitute *fines herbes* (page 13) for parsley.

❶ In medium bowl, beat butter at medium speed until smooth and creamy. Gradually add oil, beating until well blended. Beat in mustard and lemon juice. Stir in shallots, parsley and pepper. Serve at room temperature. *(Butter can be made ahead. Cover and refrigerate up to 4 days or freeze up to 6 months.)*

⅔ cup.

Preparation time: 10 minutes. Ready to serve: 10 minutes.

Per tablespoon: 90 calories, 10 g total fat (3.5 g saturated fat), 10 mg cholesterol, 70 mg sodium, 0 g fiber.

CILANTRO PESTO

Fresh chopped chiles and lime juice give a pleasant kick to cilantro pesto. Serve with tortilla chips or use to top burgers or grilled fish.

- 2 cups lightly packed fresh cilantro leaves
- ¼ cup slivered almonds, toasted*
- 1 jalapeño chile, seeded, coarsely chopped
- 2 garlic cloves, crushed
- ¼ teaspoon salt
- ¼ cup vegetable oil
- 1 tablespoon fresh lime juice
- ¼ teaspoon freshly ground pepper

❶ In food processor, combine cilantro, almonds, chile, garlic and salt; process until finely chopped. With motor running, gradually add oil through feed tube, processing until mixture forms a paste. Add lime juice and pepper; process to mix. (*Pesto can be made ahead. Place sheet of plastic wrap directly on surface to prevent discoloration; refrigerate up to 2 days or freeze up to 6 months.*)

TIP *In small, dry skillet, toast slivered almonds over medium-low heat 3 to 4 minutes or until light golden and fragrant, stirring constantly. Transfer to small bowl to cool.

2/3 cup.

Preparation time: 15 minutes. Ready to serve: 15 minutes.

Per tablespoon: 70 calories, 7 g total fat (1 g saturated fat), 0 mg cholesterol, 60 mg sodium, 0.5 g fiber.

MOROCCAN CHARMOULA SAUCE

This versatile sauce from North Africa complements grilled fish and poultry. It can also jazz up vegetarian entrées.

1½ cups lightly packed fresh cilantro leaves
1½ cups lightly packed fresh Italian parsley leaves
3 garlic cloves, crushed
1 tablespoon ground cumin
2 teaspoons paprika
¾ teaspoon salt
    Dash of cayenne pepper
½ cup vegetable or reduced-sodium chicken broth
⅓ cup reduced-fat firm silken tofu
2 tablespoons fresh lemon juice
1 tablespoon extra-virgin olive oil

❶ In food processor, combine cilantro, parsley, garlic, cumin, paprika, salt and cayenne; pulse until finely chopped. Add broth, tofu, lemon juice and oil; process until mixture forms creamy sauce, stopping to scrape down sides of bowl several times. (*Sauce can be made ahead. Place sheet of plastic wrap directly on surface to prevent discoloration; refrigerate up to 2 days.*) Just before serving, heat sauce over medium heat, stirring until heated through but not boiling.

1 cup.

Preparation time: 15 minutes. Ready to serve: 15 minutes.

Per tablespoon: 20 calories, 1.5 g total fat (0 g saturated fat), 0 mg cholesterol, 130 mg sodium, 0.5 g fiber.

PARSLEY-CAPER SAUCE

This piquant green sauce is an Italian classic. It provides a perfect flourish for grilled chicken or turkey cutlets, fish steaks or veal chops.

2   cups lightly packed fresh Italian parsley leaves
1/4   cup drained capers, rinsed
3   garlic cloves, crushed
2   tablespoons vegetable or reduced-sodium chicken broth
1   tablespoon extra-virgin olive oil
1   tablespoon low-fat mayonnaise
1   tablespoon fresh lemon juice
1   teaspoon Dijon mustard
3/4   teaspoon anchovy paste

1 In food processor, combine parsley, capers and garlic; pulse until finely chopped. Add broth, oil, mayonnaise, lemon juice, mustard and anchovy paste; process until mixture forms a creamy sauce, stopping to scrape down sides of bowl several times. (*Sauce can be made up ahead. Place sheet of plastic wrap directly on surface to prevent discoloration; refrigerate up to 2 days.*)

1/2 cup.
Preparation time: 10 minutes. Ready to serve: 10 minutes.

Per tablespoon: 30 calories, 2.5 g total fat (0.5 g saturated fat), 0 mg cholesterol, 175 mg sodium, 0.5 g fiber.

No-COOK SUMMER TOMATO SAUCE

Tomato season is all too short. Enjoy them every day in late summer. Here is an easy sauce that is only worth making with "real" tomatoes. Toss with hot pasta for a light summer supper. This is enough for about 12 ounces of uncooked pasta. Sprinkle with Parmesan if you like. Or you can use this sauce as a topping for bruschetta.

3 medium vine-ripe tomatoes, halved crosswise
3 garlic cloves, crushed,
1/2 teaspoon kosher (coarse) salt
1/8 teaspoon crushed red pepper
1 cup lightly packed fresh basil leaves, torn into 1/2-inch pieces
2 tablespoons extra-virgin olive oil
2 teaspoons balsamic vinegar, if desired
1/4 teaspoon freshly ground pepper

❶ With fingers, remove tomato seeds into strainer set over small bowl. With rubber spatula, press on seeds to extract juice. Reserve juice; dice tomatoes.

❷ Using mortar and pestle or with side of chef's knife, mash garlic, salt and red pepper into a paste.

❸ In medium bowl, combine tomatoes, reserved juice, garlic mixture, basil, oil, vinegar and pepper; toss to mix gently. Serve shortly after making. Do not refrigerate.

3 cups.

Preparation time: 20 minutes. Ready to serve: 20 minutes.

Per (3/4-cup) serving: 85 calories, 7 g total fat (1 g saturated fat), 0 mg cholesterol, 200 mg sodium, 1.5 g fiber.

CHEF'S NOTE:

• Put away your knives when you are preparing the basil. Large pieces of casually torn basil leaves are nicest for this rustic sauce.

SPRINGTIME SAUCE WITH FINES HERBES

This sauce is similar to hollandaise, but it is much lighter and easier to make. The base is actually low-fat mayonnaise that is thinned with broth, warmed and finished with fresh herbs, mustard and lemon. The sauce is perfect with poached fish.

¼ cup reduced-fat mayonnaise
¼ cup vegetable or reduced-sodium chicken broth
1 tablespoon grainy mustard
1 tablespoon extra-virgin olive oil
1 tablespoon fresh lemon juice
2 tablespoons *fines herbes* (page 13)
¼ teaspoon freshly ground pepper

❶ Place mayonnaise in small saucepan. Gradually add broth, whisking until smooth. Set saucepan over medium-low heat; cook, whisking constantly 2 to 3 minutes or until mixture is heated through but not bubbling. Remove from heat. Stir in mustard, oil, lemon juice, *Fines Herbes* and pepper. Serve warm.

¾ cup.

Preparation time: 10 minutes. Ready to serve: 15 minutes.

Per tablespoon: 30 calories, 3 g total fat (0.5 g saturated fat), 0 mg cholesterol, 65 mg sodium, 0 g fiber.

CHEF'S NOTE:

• If more convenient, use just one or two of the herbs in the *fines herbes* mixture. Or use 2 tablespoons chopped fresh dill

---

RECIPE INDEX

This index lists every recipe in Celebrating Herbs *by name. If you're looking for a specific recipe but can't recall the exact name, turn to the General Index that starts on page 173.*

GENERAL INDEX

Three ways to use this index. Find recipes by name. Or look up a main ingredient or herb and see related recipes listed. Or check out a chapter category (such as soups & stews) and see those recipes listed.